Resting In Stillness

Martin Jamyang Tenphel

&

Pema Düddul

This book first published 2020

Jalü Publications

www.jalumeditation.org

1 Lake Street, Crescent Head, New South Wales, Australia
2440

Australian National Library Cataloguing in Publication Data

A catalogue record for this book is available from the
Australian National Library

Copyright © 2020 Martin Galafassi & Dallas John Baker

All rights for this book reserved. No part of this book may
be reproduced, stored in a retrieval system, or transmitted,
in any form or by any means, electronic, mechanical,
photocopying, recording or otherwise, without the prior
permission of the copyright owner.

ISBN (13): 978-0-6483972-7-4

Dedication

Dedicated to our Heart Teachers, Togden Amtrin and Dudjom Rinpoche, Jigdral Yeshe Dorje, and to all true masters. Also to Ngakpa Karma Lhundup Rinpoche for years of friendship, support and guidance.

Contents

Acknowledgements i

Preface v

1 Sitting 1

2 Making Tea 2

3 Resting In Stillness 3

4 Too Distressed To Meditate? 4

5 Heart 8

6 Same Taste 9

7 True Compassion 10

8 Bodhichitta And Compassion 14

9 Wonder 17

10 Recognising Pure Awareness 18

11 Dealing With Difficult Times 20

12 The Incredible Jewel 22

13 The Past 23

14 Impermanence 24

15 Ground, Path And Fruit 26

16 How To Practice 30

17 The Thinking Mind 31

18 Elixir For All Ills 32

19 Sunyata (Emptiness) 34

20 Simplest Practice 36

21 Confidence 37

22 The Overactive Mind.. 44

23 Every Atom... 46

24 How To Meditate 47

25 Please, Take A Seat... 52

26 Joy... 64

27 Informal Guru Yoga 65

28 Being a Buddhist in Hell 68

29 Reach Out 74

30 There is Nothing Greater 75

31 Karma And Dzogchen.. 78

32 Cutting Through Pain.. 88

33 Sky Gazing 90

34 No Expectations... 92

35 Getting Unstuck: Troubleshooting for Committed Buddhist Practitioners.. 93

36 Meditation Traps 105

37 Simple Awareness... 108

38 Let Me Let Go 109

39 Dharmata 110

40 Home 111

41 Renunciation 112

42 Forgiveness 114

43 Concise Dakini Guru Yoga................................ 116

44 Belief And Disbelief 117

45 True Nature Of The Mind	121
46 Imminence	126
47 The Gap	127
48 Freedom From Disturbing Emotions	128
49 Simply Awaken	131
50 No Meeting Or Parting	132
51 Love Is The Ultimate Antidote	133
52 Joyful Journey	134
53 Rest the Mind	135
54 There Is Only This	136
55 Be Free In Naked Awareness	137
56 Empty Echoes	138
57 The Guru is Present Nowness	139
58 It's Up To You	140
About Pema	142
About Jamyang	143

Acknowledgements

We would like to thank all of our friends and fellow practitioners whose questions and discussions in meditation classes, mindfulness workshops and in online forums (such as our Facebook page and groups) for asking the questions and engaging in the discussions that led to the writing of the pieces in this book. Without their lively, inquisitive participation and contributions in classes, workshops and online this book would not exist. We would also like to acknowledge the kindness and wisdom of our teachers, who have answered our own questions, guided us and supported our dharma activities. Their compassion knows no bounds and for that we are exceedingly grateful.

Visit us online: www.jalumeditation.org

Yeshe Tsogyal

Preface

As Martin Jamyang Tenphel notes in the pages of this book, Buddhist practice is like making a cup of tea. We prepare by studying and contemplating the teachings, which is like putting tea and sugar in the cup. Then we pour boiling water into the cup and let it steep. The steeping process is equivalent to our meditation practice. The longer we let the tea steep, the stronger, more powerful, and more flavourful the tea will become.

What do we need to do to help the tea steep? Nothing. We just rest, relax and wait for it to do its own thing. The same goes for meditation practice. The more we practice relaxing and resting in the stillness of meditation, the more we will experience the deep satisfying joy of our true nature.

This stillness discovered in meditation, this complete relaxation, is what we have dedicated our lives to, in the hope that we might somehow use that stillness and the energy it releases to be of modest benefit to others. This was also the motivation behind writing this book.

Resting in Stillness is a collection of short pieces – essays, poems and pithy lines of advice from one practitioner to another – about the heart of the Buddhist path and especially about meditation and compassion. Many of the pieces were answers to questions posed in meditation classes at Jalü Buddhist Meditation Centre or in online discussion groups, but some are essays written in response to a need for a succinct, accessible explanation of a topic that is essential to Buddhist practice. All of the pieces are concise, grounded in experience and written in a simple, unpretentious language that we hope both beginners and advanced practitioners will appreciate.

Every word within these covers was inspired by our Buddhist teachers, our heart guides, without whom we would have no practice and no understanding of even the simplest part of the dharma, the Buddha's teachings. Jamyang's teacher, Togden Amtrin, was a revered yogi of the Drukpa Kagyu lineage. Pema's lama was Dudjom Rinpoche, Jigdral Yeshe Dorje, a revered meditation master and scholar of the Nyingma Dudjom lineage. Both Togden Amtrin and Dudjom Rinpoche are no longer physically present in the world, though we feel their presence in our lives every day. These two masters were somewhat different in their approach to teaching. Dudjom Rinpoche often shared his wisdom through writing. As his student, Pema therefore feels quite comfortable writing about the dharma. Togden Amtrin, on the other hand, usually taught directly using few words, which is the norm in the practice-oriented yogi tradition of the Drukpa lineage. As a result, Jamyang tends to share dharma with pithy insights that spontaneously arise in his mind during Guru Yoga practice. These insights arise without any conscious intent or forethought. Either way, any benefit arising from our sharing of the dharma comes directly from our gurus. Out of deep appreciation we have dedicated this book to them, even though this is not nearly enough to express our gratitude.

We hope that this little book inspires you to take the Buddhist teachings to heart, and that it supports you to settle into your practice and allow the perfect, restful stillness and joy that is your birthright to arise unhindered.

With affection,
Pema Düddul & Martin Jamyang Tenphel
(PD & MJT)
Amtrin Dudjom Ling
Crescent Head, New South Wales, Australia.
19th January 2020

Padmasambhava

1 Sitting

Meditate!
Settle the mind in deep stillness,
Dissolve the self into emptiness,
Rest in the naturally arising Great Compassion;
All confusion will be clarified.

MJT

2 Making Tea

Dharma practice is like making a cup of tea. We prepare by studying and contemplating the teachings, this is like putting tea and sugar in the cup. Then we pour boiling water into the cup and let it steep. The steeping process is equivalent to our Shamatha practice. The longer we let the tea steep, the stronger, more powerful, and more flavourful the tea will become. What do we need to do to help the tea steep? Nothing. We just rest, relax and wait for it to do its own thing. The same goes for Shamatha practice. The more we practice relaxing and resting in the stillness of Shamatha, the more we will experience the deep satisfying joy of our True Nature.

MJT

3 Resting In Stillness

By simply resting in the stillness that all of us have access to by sitting quietly, joy, peace and loving-kindness will arise naturally. Without the effort of pushing and pulling the mind this way and that, our fundamental nature, our Buddha Nature, will emerge. You need not take my word for it, test this for yourself, and you will certainly gain confidence in its veracity.

MJT

4 Too Distressed To Meditate?

There are times when the ups and downs of life take a decided dip downwards, when we feel more stressed than normal, more sad than normal, more anxious than normal. At these times we can feel totally overwhelmed. These dark periods are often precipitated by illness or loss, by grief, or simply by being worn down by an overly busy life.

At these times, those of us who are new to meditation practice can find it almost impossible to sit and find stillness. Even those with some meditation experience, with an ongoing meditation practice, can still find such times challenging. So rather than give up on spiritual practice, which in the long term produces a deep calm and inner resilience that will inoculate us from future disturbing life events, what can we do when things get rough?

If we are finding it impossible to quieten the mind, we may need a temporary, positive distraction. Mantra is good for that. When life is overwhelming and we can't sit still, reciting mantra is a good alternative. Mantra keeps us in the present moment, which is one of the key beneficial aspects of meditation. Another benefit of mantra is that, in the long run, it supports our sitting meditation indirectly, by strengthening our ability to stay in the present and focus on a single activity.

In Tibetan Buddhism there is a single mantra that is considered to contain the potency and blessing of all mantras. This is the Vajra Guru mantra:

Om Ah Hung Benzar Guru Pema Siddhi Hung

There are reasons why this mantra is useful for later, higher-level practice in Vajrayana, but for those merely wanting to use it to stay present and focussed amidst the wildness of life the precise meaning of the mantra is not so important. In fact, the mantra can often work better without a literal translation. A clear meaning for the mantra can sometimes trigger thoughts about the past and future, which is not what we want. We want to stay in the present, to use the mantra to protect the mind from its habit of wandering all over the place. Although a literal translation isn't needed, a general understanding of the mantra might be helpful. The Vajra Guru Mantra evokes our pure awakened nature, calls on our Buddha Nature to manifest. The focus of the mantra is Padmasambhava, or Guru Rinpoche, who was fully, uninhibitedly awakened. In a very real sense Guru Rinpoche and our own true nature are one and the same. The Vajra Guru mantra evokes this enlightened truth hidden beneath our dualistic mind and its constant chatter. *Om Ah Hung Benzar Guru Pema Siddhi Hung* also evokes a feeling of gratitude for Padmasambhava's teachings, the Vajrayana method that he firmly established in Tibet in the 8th century; teachings that will lead to our liberation in this very lifetime, to our recognising who we truly are.

Although it is perfectly fine to engage in positive distraction for a while, it is important to come back to our regular sitting meditation practice as soon as we can. It is also very important that we understand that the feelings we're having, the feelings of being overwhelmed, of anxiety and sadness, are utterly temporary. They are perpetuated by thoughts that, if we choose to, we can simply drop. Although the thing that will free us from these disturbing emotions is simple—merely letting go of the thoughts and beliefs that perpetuate them—it is not easy. It will take some effort. The most effective way to drop the negative thoughts perpetuating these disturbing feelings is to remember that they are impermanent, they rise like waves and then dissipate of their own accord. They also have no inherent existence. Without the energy we give them, they cannot exist. They are not a part of us. They are mere passing fictions that do not reflect our true nature at all. Every time these passing, temporary fictions arise, we need to look at them and see their impermanent and fictional nature and remind ourselves of our true nature, our fundamental goodness or Buddha Nature.

The feelings of sadness, fear and trauma and the negative thought patterns behind them are not our true nature. They are the opposite of our true nature. More to the point, the event that originally caused the trauma or sadness is gone. The past is dead. It has no power over us whatsoever. The future does not exist. There is just the present. In the present there is only pure joy and peace, albeit obscured by the temporary thoughts, feelings and emotions that we allow to continue. Even though trauma and sadness and all those disturbing emotions are not really a part of us, it is important not to underestimate the pain they cause whilst also accepting that they are not part of us and are ultimately temporary and baseless. We also need to be aware that we underestimate the profound joy and peace that is there underneath, waiting to shine through. If we just drop the beliefs and thoughts that perpetuate our disturbing and disabling emotions, that joy and peace and love becomes our reality. That is who we truly are. That is who everyone is. All sentient beings have the same profoundly pure inner nature. This brings us back to the Vajra Guru mantra, which reminds us of our profoundly pure inner nature and of Guru Rinpoche who realised that nature and taught the methods for us to do the same in a single lifetime.

Om Ah Hung Benzar Guru Pema Siddhi Hung.

While doing this mantra, we don't need to drop or do anything with our feelings. We just do the mantra. We simply repeat it silently if others are around, if we're in the supermarket say, or we can say it out loud if we're alone. If we're accumulating a certain number we can say it subvocally to speed up how many we can say per minute. No matter how or where we choose to recite the mantra, it's important to enunciate clearly so that each word is distinguishable and to keep our awareness on what we're doing, on the mantra. That way we stay in the present moment and also strengthen our attention. Make that attention gentle rather than rigid, but not so gentle that your mind wanders.

If you can find recordings or videos of your favourite mantras that you enjoy listening to, this is very good. Joy is the fuel of practice (along with enthusiasm). Resting our awareness on the sound of the mantra can be a potent form of practice. Just relax and be aware of the sound. Apart from this the only other thing I would say about mantra recitation is this: Relax. Let go. Leave the mind as it is. Actually, in all of dharma, there is nothing else beyond this.

PD

5 Heart

You may meet as many great Lamas as there are stars in the sky, but the Root Guru shines as brilliantly as the moon. You will not mistake him/her when you meet, as your heart will awaken in a way that it has never done before and will never do again.

MJT

6 Same Taste

Recognise that peace and distractions are both Empty and Emptiness itself, so learn not to prefer one over the other. Distractions are merely an illustration of the constant flux of reality, so learn to see them not as impediments, but as the path.

MJT

7 True Compassion

Compassion is the ground, the path and the fruit of the Buddhist path. It is the ground in that our true nature is ultimate compassion (Bodhichitta). It is only this true nature that enables us to become enlightened in the first place.

Compassion is the path in that it is a major component of our practice. By engaging in acts of compassion and loving kindness we connect directly with our true nature, reducing our own suffering and confusion, which in turn better equips us to assist others. This is "relative" compassion, or ordinary kindness. To be of true benefit we need Bodhichitta or "ultimate compassion", which is boundless and unbiased. We cannot truly assist others from a place of delusion or when mired in ignorance, attachment and aversion. We just can't. For this we need the awakened mind, Bodhichitta, ultimate compassion.

Compassion, in its ultimate form, is the fruit or result of the path in that when we abide permanently in our true nature (which is what enlightenment is) the only thing that manifests is unbound, limitless compassion co-emergent with the wisdom of emptiness. That is the state of awakening, which is actually nothing other than Bodhichitta.

Even though Bodhichitta is indivisible from awakening and central to the Buddhist path, it is a mistake to think that ethical action in the world (ordinary kindness) is more important than meditation, that being kind or generous is more important than sitting on the cushion. This is because these ethical actions, though certainly praise-worthy, are relative compassion, which is somewhat limited. Also, what is it that blocks true kindness from manifesting? It is dualistic mind. One of the primary tools for undoing dualistic mind and quietening our negative emotions is meditation. If we don't meditate our ordinary kindness can be blocked, and our ultimate compassion does not shine.

When we engage with the totality of the dharma for a sustained period of time we realise that the only thing that will really help others is giving rise to the enlightened mind, giving rise to *ultimate* compassion. Of course we help in the world when we can, that goes without saying. No-one is saying otherwise. Unfortunately, the ordinary help we give from a place of dualistic mind is often tainted by our self-clinging. Sometimes it feeds ego (rather than starving it) and can deepen our ignorance and, ironically, lessen our compassion in the long run.

Also, our relative actions have no guarantee of truly helping or being beneficial in a lasting way. They might help for a while and then lose their benefit, or they might not help at all. Sometimes they can actually end up making things worse. We do not have the kind of deep wisdom required to know the outcome of these kinds of actions.

It is a lack of understanding the empty and impermanent nature of things (the world and the "self" and the mind) that leads us to think that relative acts like these are more important than our meditation. We are misunderstanding what we mean by compassion. Compassion is a part of our practice, absolutely, but true compassion is much more than good deeds, especially those deeds tainted by ego. True, selfless compassion is what is important.

True compassion and meditation are of equal importance to dharma practice. However, the practice on the cushion takes precedence at first, until we are enlightened. This is because meditation practice restores us and equips us to deal with the suffering of the world and thus continue to help in the limited ways we can. Relative compassion is the dharma practice that we do when we can, when we have the capacity and when the opportunity arises.

Meditation on the other hand must be a way of life, a daily practice that we never miss no matter what is going on in our lives.

It is really important that we get this: the difference between ego-based "meritorious deeds" and Bodhichitta and the equal importance of true compassion and meditation practice. The meditation we each do is in fact a form of true compassion, one that leads to awakening.

Actively helping others without ego, without thinking we're good people for doing it, is also true compassion. To negate one for the other is not helpful in the long run. We need both, true, selfless compassion and the wisdom of emptiness that arises in meditation. We cannot attain realisation without each of them together.

In fact, when we practice true compassion, because it is of the same taste as the awakened mind, it leads to a realisation of emptiness. Likewise, when we meditate on emptiness, it leads to the dawning of true compassion. They are intrinsically linked; or, more precisely, they are in essence one and the same. This is because they are both coming from a place of non-self, a place in which the ego is abandoned.

In contrast, ordinary kindness is very much part of dualistic mind. The quote below makes the connection between true compassion and wisdom of emptiness very clear:

> Practising compassion will bring about the recognition of emptiness as the true nature of the mind. When you practice virtuous actions of love and compassion on the relative level, you spontaneously realize the profound nature of emptiness, which is the absolute level. In turn, if you focus your meditation practice on emptiness, then your loving kindness and compassion will spontaneously grow. These two natures, the absolute and the relative, are not opposites; they always arise together. They have the same nature; they are inseparable like a fire and its heat or the sun and its light. Compassion and emptiness are not like two sides of a coin. Emptiness and

compassion are not two separate elements joined together; they are always coexistent.[1]

All the enlightened beings of the past and all the realised masters of the present repeatedly point out that a complete dharma practice should be our priority, one with an equal emphasis on true, selfless compassion and meditation. These things always go together, always. That being said, full awakening, the dawning of Bodhichitta, which is ultimate compassion inseparable from the wisdom of emptiness, is not possible without first taming the mind through a daily meditation practice. Thus it is clear that meditation is the foundation of both true compassion and wisdom.

PD

---

[1] Khenchen Palden Sherab Rinpoche & Khenpo Tsewang Dongyal Rinpoche, in *The Buddhist Path*.

8 Bodhichitta And Compassion

To begin with, Bodhicitta is distinct from the experience of ordinary kindness and compassion, because the experience of Bodhicitta is completely free of a sense of Self. Whilst ordinary kindness and compassion are incredibly important, they still involve a sense of the "I", and thus are not totally free of self-clinging or a sense that "I" am doing this for an "other".

Bodhicitta arises in one's heart whenever we come into contact with our True Nature, our Buddha Nature. There are many practices that assist a practitioner to experience Bodhicitta, and for me, it has been through either resting in the deep stillness that comes from Shamatha meditation practice, or when experiencing deep devotion towards my Guru.

The experience of Bodhicitta at its peak is one of tremendously blissful love and compassion towards all living beings; humans, animals, insects, every living creature without any discrimination in your mind at all between any of them. The experience is felt very strongly in the area of the heart and is a blazing all-encompassing love towards all beings equally. During the experience there's not the slightest differentiation between the wish for friends, enemies and strangers alike to have everything that they could possibly need to be free of all of their suffering.

Because there is no sense of Self while Bodhicitta blazes, ones heart and mind become completely open, and one experiences a vast and spacious awareness, totally infused with tremendous love and a sense of Oneness with all beings. With no sense of Self, you feel no seperation between yourself and other beings.

Initially, we train in experiencing Bodhicitta while doing some kind of practice, but eventually you feel Bodhicitta start to arise little by little outside of your practice sessions in your daily life. Our training then becomes to continue to deepen our experience of Bodhicitta until it remains in our hearts at all times, and in all situations.

Bodhicitta thus becomes the ultimate expression of accomplishment for a practitioner, and is the fruit that will help you become tremendously beneficial to others. In real world terms, you will start to recognise that Bodhicitta has an effect on those around you, when you start to notice that others feel an inexplicable trust in you and an ease around you. As an example, wild animals such as birds may not exhibit their instinctual innate fear around you, and may begin to engage with you in a familiar and trusting manner. They may begin to feel comfortable coming closer to you to be fed or just to rest nearby, knowing somehow that you won't harm them. You will begin to see more and more little signs of how Bodhicitta radiates outwards from you and affects others in a subtle and positive way.

For a highly realised being, or a Buddha, their blazing Bodhicitta makes them a beacon of trust and light to the world around them. Jetsunma Tenzin Palmo told me how my own Lama, Togden Amtrin, was like a "Universal Grandfather" (as she called him), to the community of Tashijong where he lived. Everybody in the community, whether they were a High Lama, a great Yogi, a regular monk or nun, or a member of the lay community, felt comfortable to go and see him and tell him of their needs or problems. And as one who was permanently imbued with great Bodhicitta, he was always ready to offer prayers for a sickness, advice on family problems, or give direct teachings on the Nature of Mind, the ultimate cure for all samsaric suffering.

To conclude, the only way for a practitioner to show that their practice is working, is through the demonstration of

Bodhicitta, or acts of selfless kindness and compassion. One may have done thousands of hours of meditation, taken all kinds of high teachings and empowerments from many great Lamas, visited many holy sites on pilgrimage, and so on, but the only actual tangible visible way to demonstrate that you are a true practitioner of the Buddhas teachings is by displaying Bodhicitta in daily life. Ultimately, things like great meditative experiences, amazing visions and tremendous bliss don't amount to anything if you can't be selflessly kind and compassionate to those you meet on a daily basis.

MJT

9 Wonder

Leave room in your mind for wonder to arise! Don't suffocate your practice with too many concepts and expectations. Tremendous beauty, joy and freedom will emerge naturally if you leave space for it to do so.

MJT

10 Recognising Pure Awareness

For those practitioners who are not able to meditate regularly, there are other ways to train in recognition of pure awareness. Simply recognising single moments of basic awareness is the way to begin. In moments of surprise or shock or great bliss our conceptual mind falls away. These are moments we can train in the recognition of pure awareness. In moments like these we are so shocked or pleased or blissed out that, before we have a chance to react with fear or clinging or outrage, our conceptual mind falls away, thus giving us a moment of pure awareness. Pure Nowness. Total presentness.

This is why practises like Chod are a method to recognize and train in pure awareness, rigpa. Every beat of the drum is a moment of pure awareness, every ring of the bell is a moment of pure awareness, every gap of silence between the sound of the drum and bell is a moment of pure awareness.

If you can keep your mind from jumping in and commenting and assessing everything, there are infinite moments of pure awareness to recognise. In ordinary life, hearing a screaming child is an opportunity to recognise that moment of pure awareness before worry or irritation arise. A sip of tea is an opportunity to recognise that moment of rigpa. Hearing the ocean is an opportunity to recognise that moment of pure awareness. Feeling a cool wind on your skin, or water on your hands is a moment of pure awareness, if you don't jump in with the conceptual mind.

The more you train on the cushion, whether it be in meditation or Chod, the more you will learn to recognise these glimpses of pure awareness, rigpa. Then, when you go and do regular activities you start to recognise brief moments of rigpa, through sounds, smells, tastes, touch, thoughts and sights.

Illness and pain are acute moments of potentiality to recognise awareness. These are often impossible for us to ignore because of their severity, but they are acute moments that can help train us in recognition of basic awareness, if we learn not to meet the experience with immediate aversion.

If we can just say, "Oh, hello pain, it's you again, just a moment of basic awareness", then this can propel our practice forward."

MJT

11 Dealing With Difficult Times

If you spend any time on social media at all, you will have noticed that each and every day people are asking their "friends" for ideas on how to cope with the myriad of negative stuff that's happening in the world today. The vast majority of people who do offer advice are suggesting external changes that may, perhaps, help temporarily. Rarely does anyone mention anything that would affect lasting change, such as practising Dharma. Few, if any, suggest that the change needs to come from within. Some people suggest that being kinder might help, which is dharma in a simple way and is, of course, very good.

Sadly, no-one ever comes close to suggesting that if we dedicate our lives to working towards realisation through practising meditation and understanding impermanence and emptiness, and then helping others to do the same, we'd see a totally different external reality, a totally different world. Why is it that so few people understand that looking inward and developing inner peace, love and joy will change the outer world radically for the better? Why is that most people just want to keep tinkering with their external reality, as humans have done forever? It's simply because that is their habit and they are ignorant of any other alternative. How have these habits worked out for them so far? It hasn't been of any benefit at all. The world is still the same, full of suffering, hatred and fear. It's quite frustrating and saddening to see so many people just not understanding the true importance of Dharma practice on a global scale, and what it's real worth and potential is.

For those of us who do value this kind of inward action

that will lead to real lasting change, it feels like we're shouting into the void with our attempts to support others to engage with the Dharma. Whenever a problem arises, most people instantly look outwards for a solution, and never inwards. The habitual way people attempt to deal with the challenges we all face is actually at the root of the problem. Given this, those who do understand the value of inner change need to highlight for everyone around them that deep, lasting external change begins with focusing seriously on internal change. We also need to do the practice ourselves to set an example. This is in fact how we deal with the myriad of negative stuff we face each day: by looking inwards, by sitting in meditation, by understanding the impermanent and empty nature of all things and encouraging others to do the same. If we do this, we will be transformed, we will acquire an inner peace and joy that will radiate out into the external world. As we change, the world will change. Therefore, our priority must be the inner practice of meditation. Be kind, of course. Be generous, of course. Be ethical, of course. Be patient, of course. Take action to help others when you can, of course. These are all important aspects of the Dharma, but they will have a limited reach if they are not grounded in a deep understanding of impermanence and emptiness and powered by the stillness and insight that can only be found in meditation.

To really help others you must first liberate yourself. A person trapped in a burning house cannot help others escape if they themselves are blindfolded. Take off the blindfold. See the true nature of the mind and all things, only then will you be able to save others.

MJT & PD

12 The Incredible Jewel

Bodhicitta is like an incredible jewel with many amazing facets. One of these facets is feeling gratitude for what we have. On an outer level we can feel grateful for things like this human life, food and shelter. On an inner level, we can feel grateful for meeting the Dharma, meeting great Masters and learning practices that will lead to Liberation. The more you practice, the more gratitude will well up from deep within you for all the great and small things in this world.

MJT

13 The Past

Don't let the past ruin your present and your future. Whether you experienced a hurtful or traumatic event 20 years ago, or 20 minutes ago, as soon as negative emotions arise in response to its memory, apply the antidote, return to the present moment, and move forward. The Dharma offers many antidotes, and each practitioner will have an affinity with at least one. You may find bringing your awareness back to the breath most helpful, or reciting some mantra, or meditating on loving kindness and Compassion, or recalling the face of your beloved Teacher. Whichever you choose does not matter, as long as it pulls you out of the past and back into the present. Remember, the past is dead and gone, so do not let it destroy your present and future peace of mind.

We all have bad days from time to time, but it's important to remember that the past is truly dead, and the future does not yet exist. So where does this leave us? With the opportunity to rest in spacious awareness right now!

MJT

14 Impermanence

Impermanence. It's a vast topic, with so many implications, but these are just two little tips to help you contemplate impermanence:

1. We start by observing impermanence in simple ways in the external world. The changing nature of things like the weather and the seasons are obvious illustrations of the impermanent nature of the world we live in. Observe the constant flux of things moving, altering, and transitioning from one state to another.

2. Then turn this understanding inwards towards the mind. Recognise that our minds are also in constant flux. Always a new thought, a new mood, a new desire, a new aversion.
Observe the transient and temporary nature of thoughts, emotions, feelings, perceptions. See how utterly impermanent this thing we call mind is. You will see that it's completely unstable and has no permanent characteristics.
When we contemplate in this way, we ultimately come to the understanding that our identities, our "self", and all that we believe we are, is in reality a totally unstable and impermanent illusion.
Once we develop a deep understanding of impermanence, this will lead us very easily to an understanding of Emptiness, which is that all things, external and internal, are free from any inherent qualities or characteristics; that everything, from our external physical realities to our minds themselves, are completely empty of

any stable, permanent or solid nature.

Thus we can see, that a realisation of impermanence is so incredibly important to free ourselves from entanglement in this temporary experience that we call Samsara.

MJT

15 Ground, Path And Fruit

I would like to share a short teaching from a great Nyingma meditation master. The teaching is from a poem called "Prayer of the Ground, Path, and Fruit" by the extraordinary Mipham Rinpoche (1846-1912). The teaching as a whole discourages learning by rote, forced styles of meditation, and the empty performance of ceremonies and rituals. I would like to share just two of the stanzas from that poem. Here they are:

> Present since the beginning,
> it is not dependent upon being cultivated,
> Nor upon such things as differences in one's capacity.
>
> May this vital point of mind,
> not trusted since it seems too easy,
> Be recognised through the power of the master's oral instructions.
>
> To elaborate or to examine is nothing but adding concepts.
> To make effort or to cultivate is only to exhaust oneself.
> To focus or to concentrate is but a trap of further entanglement.
> May these painful fabrications be cut from within.

These two stanzas are perhaps the most powerful from Mipham Rinpoche's poem as teaching. The first stanza points out some important characteristics of the nature of one's mind (one's fundamental goodness as it were). The second stanza elaborates on the methodology for apprehending (or discovering/abiding in) the nature of mind.

The first stanza says quite strongly that one's Buddha nature does not need to be cultivated. We do not need to perform multiple repetitions of practices in order to grow, develop or improve our Buddha nature. Our Buddha nature is as it is. It does not need to be improved.

Buddha Nature is not like a muscle that needs to be developed. It is more like a golden nugget hidden under our bed. All we need to do is to see it - and that is achieved by simply knowing that it's there. In other words, if we familiarise ourselves with the fact that there is this nugget, and that it's hidden very close to us, we can then take it out and enjoy its beauty. We need to familiarise ourselves with the notion of our own Buddha Nature, and the fact that it abides with us always, but is merely temporarily out of view.

Also, this first stanza indicates that this Dzogchen method of doing things—some simple contemplation into the nature of mind supported by some basic study into that nature, and some simple actions (effortless meditation) to bring the nugget out from its hiding place—are not only for those of 'high capacity'. Mipham Rinpoche makes it quite clear that capacity has nothing to do with it – the fundamental nature of all beings is the same.

The second stanza outlines the main obstacles to experiencing our own nature directly. To philosophise or theorise is the first obstacle. This is why 'simple study' on the fundamental topics of impermanence and emptiness is emphasised.

Furthermore, to engage in multiple repetitions of 'virtuous' activities and 'merit producing' practices is merely to exhaust oneself, it will not necessarily be of benefit in the immediate moment. To focus or engage in forced concentrative meditation is also an obstacle – the kind of mind required for this is the totally relaxed mind that experiences its own nature directly.

I really feel that I've been harping on about this point for decades but: The purpose of Dharma practice is to experience one's true face, to discover and abide in the true nature, the empty nature that we call Buddha Nature. The swiftest way to achieve that purpose is to engage in some simple study (or rather informed contemplation) around the nature of mind (emptiness), to engage in some simple shamatha style meditation and to cultivate a totally relaxed attitude to all phenomena.

The purpose of dharma is *not* to accumulate hundreds of thousands of repetitions of a certain practice, or to collect empowerments, or to get fancy titles like lama or khenpo or rinpoche. In my humble opinion no practice or 'spiritual' endeavour should be undertaken unless it supports this greater goal.

For myself, I find that some repetitious behaviour (reciting mantra) is calming and facilitates a more relaxed attitude and helps me to remain in the moment. So I do it. On the other hand, lots of repetitions of complex practices in groups doesn't do that for me so I tend not to do that. But let me stress, it's all about *you*.

Whatever supports us to abide completely in our own fundamental nature then that's what we should do. Many Masters have said that only we will know what that is. No Lama can tell us what is best for us, we must determine that for ourselves. Of course, it's good to be informed and so the guidance of Masters does have an important place in our spiritual lives.

Without my own Masters I couldn't have written a single word of this chapter, and I certainly would not be practising in the way that I am now. Much of the joy of my life comes directly from this practice and so I owe much of my happiness to these Masters. On the other hand, without my own intelligence, my own effort, my own heart, my own Buddha Nature, no path (and no awakening) is possible either.

To summarise, and to make the same point again: relax, do a little simple study into the impermanent and empty nature of mind (and all phenomena) and a little gentle shamatha meditation each and every day.

Otherwise, just enjoy life and the clarity of mind by relaxing into the true nature, just as it is.

PD

16 How To Practice

When it comes to Buddhist practice, it's not what you do, but how you do it. If you practice with a mind that's cold and hard as ice, you'll get nowhere. If you practice with a heart as warm and soft as fresh baked bread, you'll definitely experience the blessings of Buddha's teachings.

MJT

17 The Thinking Mind

I have come to really understand this through my meditation, and gain real conviction in it: One does not need the thinking mind, thought, the intellect, to achieve realisation. This thinking, analysing, conceptual mind is far more of a hindrance than a help. One achieves realisation by fully engaging with the heart; by fully opening the heart. The experience of Buddha Nature arises in the heart. The experience of Bodhicitta arises in the heart. The vast spacious awareness is experienced in the heart.

So, leave all your thoughts alone. They aren't your friends, and most importantly they aren't YOU. They just keep you ensnared in the endless activities of the mind. Let it all go. There's nothing to do but rest in the wide openness that already exists in the centre of your heart, and allow your Buddha Nature to bloom.

MJT

18 Elixir For All Ills

The best meditation posture is stillness. In meditation and when at ease, make the stillness of the body your object. Focus awareness on the body. *Feel* the stillness of the body. Rest in the stillness of the body. Then simply be aware of the stillness of the body and remain in the now.

If there is tension or pain in the body, simply reconnect with the stillness of the body. Do this again and again, always gently. Then be aware of the greater stillness deep within and gradually drop the object and the observer. Innate Awareness remains. Rest there.

The best mantra is silence. In meditation and when at ease, make the silence of speech your object. Focus awareness on silence. *Listen* to the silence, *hear* the silence. Then simply be aware of the silence. Rest in the silence and remain in the now.

If there is noise, simply reconnect with the silence. Place your awareness on the silence beyond sound. Do this again and again, always gently. Then be aware of the greater silence deep within and gradually drop the object and the observer. Innate Awareness remains. Rest there.

The mind is best left alone in total relaxation. In meditation and when at ease, make the boundless spaciousness of mind your object. *Feel* the openness and spaciousness of the mind and heart. Rest in the spaciousness of mind and remain in the now. Then simply be aware of this spaciousness, luminous and open.

If there is thought, simply reconnect with the spaciousness. Place your awareness on the spaciousness. Do this again and again, always gently. Then be aware of the greater spaciousness within and gradually drop the object and the observer. Innate Awareness remains. Rest there.

Rest in stillness. Rest in silence. Rest in spaciousness. In meditation and when at ease, rest in Innate Awareness.

PD

19 Sunyata (Emptiness)

Emptiness is both a much misunderstood and much overused term. In English 'emptiness' is a word often used to describe an unfortunate human condition typified by disturbing feelings of emotional numbness and purposelessness. Any dictionary shows as synonyms for emptiness the words barrenness, blankness, and worthlessness. In Buddhism, the word emptiness has nothing to do with emotional dysfunction or worthlessness. Given these negative connotations perhaps 'emptiness' is not the best word to use in this sense but as there is now a long tradition of its use it seems we might be stuck with it. Here, however, I will use the original Sanskrit term, Sunyata (pronounced *shunyata*), as it doesn't have any negative connotations.

Despite a plethora of written commentaries and oral teachings on Sunyata even long-term Buddhists often misuse or misunderstand the term. Many believe that it means that nothing really exists. On the other hand people throw it around as though it is a magical incantation that refutes or equalizes everything: everything is emptiness, everything is emptiness. Both of these attitudes are not in line with the dharma as Shakyamuni Buddha taught it more than two thousand years ago. The truth of Sunyata is not that nothing exists, but that nothing exists in the way we think it does. To put it very simply, the word Sunyata is an umbrella term that points to some characteristics of reality, phenomena and the world that are, though usually hidden to our dualistic minds, rather wonderful.

On the simplest level it means the following things. All

phenomena—including our personalities, our thoughts and feelings—are *impermanent* and changeable. Sunyata implies dynamism and flux. The term Sunyata also points to the fact that all phenomena only exist in *mutual interdependence* with all other phenomena and therefore are never wholly self-sufficient. In this sense it implies interconnectedness.

Sunyata also means that phenomena are devoid (empty) of an irreducible identity or essence. Things, including ourselves, only *seem* to have inherent existence because of misperception. Based on that misperception we apply labels or names to things that, in effect, give the impression that they are separate, permanent, and independent. This is what we Buddhists call *delusion*; the belief in separately existing, permanent things, especially a separate, permanent and independently existing "self". This is the biggest delusion. The belief in a separately existing, permanent, independent and innate identity or 'self' leads to the separation of self and other, and that inevitably leads to attachment or attraction and aversion or dislike. From there we get all the unhelpful emotions, like fear, anger and hatred. Conversely, understanding Sunyata leads to a sense of freedom, connection, joy and limitless potential. The direct experience of emptiness is an experience of oneness, openness and spontaneity.

PD

20 Simplest Practice

Being a practitioner is like having a very obscure hobby. When you find someone else who is interested in it, it's exciting. Most people these days know a bit about basic Buddhist principles, but when you start to talk about practice the conversation ends because most people just aren't doing it. I've always been really focused on getting to the absolute heart and pith of things when it comes to the Dharma, so over the years I've whittled my practice down to the absolute heart essence practices.

I only have one heart practice, which is Guru Yoga, and then shamatha (meditation) practice. That's it for me. I've found that this is all I need. I won't ever need anything else. In my lineage, the Drukpa, and in Pema Duddul's lineage, the Nyingma, these practices lead ultimately to the practice of Dzogchen. By getting solid foundational knowledge and practice experience in these two things our mind will be ripe when we get to the point when we are ready to practice Dzogchen.

So for me, practice is about simplifying and stripping the mind back to its bare bones so that one can eventually train in resting in the Nature of Mind. If we clutter the mind up with decades of acquiring many complicated practices that we don't actually need, we might have trouble when it comes time to drop everything in the Dzogchen view.

MJT

21 Confidence

In my personal experience many Western Dharma practitioners are riddled with low self-esteem and a profound lack of spiritual confidence. Self-loathing is an acute form of suffering. Often we think that, because it is directed inwards, self-loathing is more or less benign. This is far from the case.

Self-loathing, low self-esteem and lack of confidence undermine our spiritual practice by weakening our belief in our ability to embody the purity of the dharma. If we have no confidence in our ability to realise the path, we quite simply *won't* realise the path. Lack of confidence blocks our enlightenment and, by extension, cuts off our ability to help others by preventing us from attaining the wisdom to discern between truly beneficial action and action that, though perhaps temporarily helpful, is ultimately of no significant benefit.

A clear and direct antidote to low self-esteem and lack of confidence is the profound teachings on Buddha nature. The Buddha Nature teachings do no less than show us our own true nature. As Khenchen Thrangu Rinpoche writes in *The Three Vehicles of Buddhist Practice*:

> Those who heed the Buddha's teachings can discover this incomparable thing which has been within us all the time and which we never knew was there until we were told. For that essence to be revealed we need to meditate on the truth, on the essence of phenomena, the way things really are. If we do that we clean away all the delusions and defilements which have been covering up that essence.

It cannot be put more simply: our true nature is the Buddha nature, the stainless awareness that is the *Great Perfection*. As the Hevajra Tantra states:

> Sentient beings are Buddhas, but they are temporarily obscured.
> Once this obscuration is removed, they are Buddhas indeed.
> The Body of the Supreme Buddha is all-pervading,

The Uttaratantra (Verse 27) puts it this way:

> The Absolute is one undifferentiated Whole
> And the potential of Buddhahood exists in every living being.
> Therefore, for ever and anon, all that lives
> Is endowed with the Essence of the Buddha.

We must, therefore, focus strongly on developing an unshakeable confidence in this Buddha nature. This should be the starting point for Western Dharma practitioners in particular. Many Westerners fail to progress on the path because they have no confidence in their own capacity, their own true nature. They are doing what they always do, looking outwards, mesmerised by the cultural trappings of Vajrayana, the bells and whistles (or the bells, drums and thighbone trumpets), rather than what we need to do to be free of dualistic mind – look quietly inwards, gently but persistently, each and every day. We need to connect with the essence of the Buddhist teachings and the essence of ourselves.

The essence is the pristine nature, or innate natural awareness (rigpa), which is not impacted by time, culture or mindset. It is timelessly pure and accessible to us all through the simple meditation practices first taught some 2600 years ago by the Buddha. We don't need an array of complicated visualisation (or yidam) practices or difficult yogic exercises. Once we have some confidence in that essence, in Buddha nature, then achieving a direct experience of the pristine nature, and learning to rest in it, becomes possible in this lifetime. It will also make all those other practices unnecessary.

The only essential (and guaranteed) method is to develop certainty, absolutely doubtless trust, about our own fundamental goodness, which is also the ultimate nature of all things, and to then directly experience that nature and abide in it. This is achieved in simple silent sitting meditation when underpinned by and understating of our primordial purity and the true nature of all things, which is called the View (*tawa*).

It seems to me that so much of what hinders us arises from our deeply-rooted lack of confidence and lack of experience in the very simple meditation practice that will reveal the pristine nature of mind. It is widely understood by Himalayan meditation masters, especially those teaching in the West, that when Westerners are taught about their deep potential they cannot believe it. If they can conceive of enlightenment at all, they tend to think it is only possible for a rare and special few, mostly the Tibetan masters of the past. His Holiness the Fourteenth Dalai Lama has often spoken about the lack of self-esteem and self-respect that he sees in many people in the modern, Western world. One lama has said that underlying Western dharma students' whole outlook is a neurotic conviction of their own limitations. There is an evident tendency for Westerners to flock to Asian dharma teachers and ignore Western ones. This is both a kind of internalised racism that suggests that Westerners cannot be authentic dharma teachers, cannot be realised, but also a reflection of their lack of trust in their own fundamental nature. They project this self-loathing outwards onto those who look and act like them, other Westerners. This conviction that Westerners cannot be truly realised will impede the awakening of those who fall prey to it, as I already mentioned earlier, because it totally undermines their understanding of the heart or quintessence of the Buddha's teaching: that we all have

Buddha nature, that all sentient beings are essentially perfect as they are irrespective of gender, race, ethnicity, sexuality or species. As Tsele Natsok Rangdrol (born 1608) wrote long ago:

> The quintessence of the meaning of all the infinite and countless teachings of the Buddhas is that the wisdom essence of the tathagatas is present as the nature of sentient beings. The innumerable different kinds of dharma teachings and vehicles are indeed only taught for the purpose of realizing this nature.[2]

When we start talking about ourselves as being 'already perfect' or the same as a Buddha a risk sometimes arises – we might think we can do whatever we like, no matter how it affects others. We might begin to think we're like gods or, worse still, that we do not need to be careful about the impact of our actions. Much of the risk associated with discussions of Buddha Nature in a theistic environment, a culture ignorant of Sunyata, is ameliorated by the very mundane fact that most Westerners who are drawn to Buddhism are raised and live in a secular culture. Most of them are agnostics or atheists with little or no belief in theism, in god. With a basic introduction to the concepts of Sunyata most Westerners can discuss Buddha Nature without falling into the traps of theism or spiritual arrogance.

Given that lack of confidence is often our main obstacle or limitation, then it seems prudent to focus on the only known antidote to that – contemplation on the Buddha nature. That said, it is wise to heed the advice of Padmasambhava, the eighth century yogi who established Buddhism in Tibet, when he said of his own practice: 'Although my view is higher than the sky, my respect for the cause and effect of actions is as fine as grains of flour'.

---

[2] From *Lamp of Mahamudra*, Shambhala publications, page 1. Translated by Erik Pema Kunsang.

Taking this advice to heart means to contemplate and realise the truth of Sunyata and Buddha nature while also living a highly ethical life characterised by humility and simplicity.

So many great Buddhist teachers of the past have exhorted us to have confidence in the *path*, which is the practice of the dharma itself, to have confidence in the result or *fruit*, which is enlightenment or Buddhahood, and, perhaps most importantly, to have confidence in the *ground* or view which is our pristine nature. Our own potential for enlightenment only exists because our fundamental nature is exactly the same as the Buddha's fundamental nature.

Development of confidence in our own potential, the Buddha nature, has been largely ignored in the West as the focus of our practice. This is perhaps due to the fact that many of us have been led to believe that we are confident enough already, perhaps *too* confident. There is an idea circulating in the dharma scene that Westerners are arrogant and proud and that our first priority must be to undermine these negative emotions. In my personal experience, truly arrogant people are reasonably rare. This is not to say that arrogance is not an issue for practitioners in the West but rather that it is likely no larger a problem than in Asia. In the West, what we often describe as pride is really *false-pride*, something that wounded people have developed to cover up a more painful emotion that lies underneath it – which is usually self-loathing.

In psychiatry and psychology this process is well understood. It is known in psychoanalysis as *compensation* or as *reaction formation*. Basically, when we have a feeling or thought that we find too disturbing to experience we do whatever we can not to feel it. One way we avoid these unbearable feelings is to develop another one to cover-up or compensate for them. So, if we have low self-esteem, if we feel inferior to others, we generate a feeling of superiority. This second feeling, because it is projected outwards and not inwards as self-loathing is, is much easier to endure and may even bring us some temporary relief.

Unfortunately any positive effect this process of compensation brings is very flimsy and vanishes the minute something, or someone, triggers the underlying feelings of inferiority. Then we get angry or depressed, because we are afraid that we are going to have to feel that self-loathing and, perhaps worse, we are terrified that others may see us in the way we see ourselves: as pathetic, worthless and unlovable.

As I already mentioned, self-loathing is an acute and debilitating form of suffering. We have a tendency to ignore it, thinking it benign, but for many of us it is *the* most serious threat to the stability of our dharma practice and our future realisation. It is worth repeating that if we have no confidence in our ability to realise the path we quite simply *won't* realise the path. We will undermine ourselves, or self-sabotage, at every step of the way. Without confidence we are prevented from developing the ability to help others. Our practice is stalled and we do not develop the wisdom of discernment – the ability to truly assist others by choosing action that is ultimately beneficial over action that is only partially beneficial or worse, actually harmful in the long run.

What we need is not ordinary but *Vajra* confidence, which is confidence not in the dualistic mind, the ego and our deluded identities, but in the Buddha Nature. Without Vajra confidence, without certainty in our Buddha Nature (our inner perfection and irreducible potential) then how can we ever recognise, let alone express, our ultimate pristine nature? Mostly we just hope that our low self-esteem, our self-hatred, will just go away by itself. This is never going to happen.

On the upside, as with all other things, our self-loathing is empty of inherent existence, which means that it depends on causes and conditions to exist. This is good news. It means that we can capitalise on the inbuilt dynamism of reality—Sunyata or emptiness—and change the characteristics of our mind. We can dissolve the self-loathing by undermining its causes and conditions. The principle way we do this is by developing an understanding of the Buddha Nature, the pristine nature that we share with all beings and all things. We dissolve our current beliefs about who and what we are, which are the causes for our self-hatred, by developing an understanding about our true and pristine nature. We also remove the condition in which these negative beliefs about ourselves thrive – which is the delusion that things exist in and of themselves in a permanent way. We destroy the belief that if we feel a thing it must be both legitimate and permanent. Instead, we understand that our mind is dynamic and changeable, or empty. Our feelings and beliefs can be changed as easily as we change our clothes. Most of all we recognise that we and all sentient beings are in all respects equal to the Buddha.

We are equal to the Buddha, yes, indubitably, but so is everyone else, including our so-called enemies. We have the Buddha Nature, undeniably, but so does a cow, a bird and a mosquito. Gaining absolute conviction in this is our only hope for awakening.

PD

22 The Overactive Mind

For those who think they have an overactive mind: No-one truly has an overactive mind. The true nature of the mind is calm and clear, like the waters of a pristine and still lake.

If you take a glass of that water and it has sediment in it, what do you do to make it clear? Nothing. You leave it alone and it will settle naturally. If you keep stirring it, it will never settle.

Giving the mind things to do in meditation is just stirring it up. Leave the mind alone. Just let it settle. You need do nothing more than place your awareness gently on your breath and the mind will settle, in time. And that's the thing you need - to spend more time in practice. If you find your mind is not settling, it means you need to sit longer.

Don't turn it into an extreme sport, some kind of endurance thing, it should always be relaxed, but make sure you sit for at least 30 minutes each and every day. If you do that, you will see that the mind will settle and you will gain confidence in the true nature of your mind - that perfect clarity and calmness.

We need a daily meditation practice because, if we only meditate irregularly, the time it takes for the mind to settle will never shorten. If we have a daily meditation practice the time it takes for the mind to settle gets shorter and shorter. You will see if you have a break from your meditation practice, your mind will take longer to settle again. We need to be persistent and consistent.

Furthermore, if you are having trouble settling in to a regular practice routine, this is likely because you have not developed an understanding of impermanence. If you understand impermanence, you will be driven to practice.

Finally, we need to trust that the mind, beneath all that dualistic overthinking, is naturally calm, naturally lucid. That trust in itself helps to settle the mind, to reveal that it really is calm and clear in essence.

MJT & PD

23 Every Atom

The Enlightened Nature exists within every atom and cell of your being. It exists within every moment of awareness and every movement of mind. This is who you truly are.

MJT

24 How To Meditate

What follows are basic tips to meditation practice for absolute beginners. The form of meditation described here is that common to the Drukpa Kagyu and Nyingma traditions of Tibetan Buddhism. I'd like to start with a quote from Dudjom Rinpoche, Jigdral Yeshe Dorje, one of the greatest meditators of the twentieth century:

> Although hundreds or thousands of explanations are given,
> There is only one thing to be understood:
> Know the one thing that liberates everything,
> Awareness itself, your true nature.[3]

View

As the quote above shows, the most important practice in Buddhism is experiencing the true nature of mind. This can only be done in meditation. Meditation is most fruitful when it is supported by two things: Renunciation and a basic knowledge of Sunyata or emptiness. We especially need to grasp the empty nature of mind. Contemplating emptiness regularly will support our meditation practice.

In a Buddhist context, renunciation means to turn our minds away from anything that blocks or delays our ability to experience the true nature of mind. Buddhists see three things as the main problem: attachment, sometimes called desire or craving; aversion, sometimes called anger or hate; and ignorance, which means, basically, not understanding Sunyata or emptiness.

---

[3] From *Wisdom Nectar: Dudjom Rinpoche's Heart Advice*

Put simply, Sunyata means that all things are interconnected, interdependent, impermanent and are devoid of any lasting, intrinsic self-nature or essence. We don't need to obsess over this idea, we don't need to do huge amounts of intellectual fussing and study, we just need to accept and understand in what ways things are impermanent, in what ways tings are interdependent, and in what ways things lack an inherent self-nature.

Posture
When we think about meditation, we think in terms of postures; postures of body, speech and mind. In other words, what we do with our body, what we do with our speech and what we do with our mind.

According to Padmasambhava, who established Buddhism in Tibet 1200 years or so ago, the best meditation posture for the body is the one that is most comfortable for you, so long as the spine is more or less straight. The best posture for speech is silence. Or as Padmasambhava put it, the best mantra is silence. The best mental attitude is to simply let the mind be, to allow it to relax into its natural state. The physical posture we most often use in meditation is:

- Spine more or less straight;
- Eyes open but half-lidded, gently looking at the space a few feet in front;
- Tongue is curled so that its tip touches the roof of the mouth just behind the teeth;
- The mouth is relaxed and lips slightly open;
- Hands are laid flat, palms down, on the thighs or knees.

In his *Stages of Meditation*, Kamalashila (740-795) writes:

> Then, they should seat themselves on a comfortable seat, either in the full lotus posture of Vairochana or the half-lotus posture. Their eyes should not be open too wide, nor too tightly closed, but focused on the tip of the nose. Their body should not be bent forward or backward, but

kept straight, and their attention turned inwards. Their shoulders should rest evenly, and the head should not be tilted back or forward or to either side. The nose should be in line with the navel. The teeth and lips should rest in their natural state, and the tongue should touch the upper palate. Inhalation and exhalation should be just barely discernible, gentle, soft and natural, without undue noise, effort or agitation.

If that posture does not feel comfortable, you can meditate with eyes closed and tongue just resting on the floor of the mouth with lips closed.

Padmasambhava gave this simple four part instruction on how to practice meditation:
1. Don't dwell on the past
2. Don't anticipate the future
3. Remain in the present moment
4. Leave the mind alone.

These are pretty straight-forward instructions. In terms of the third one *Remaining in the present moment*, if our attention is on our breathing, we are already in the present moment. Nothing else to do. There is no past or future if we are focussed on our breath.

In terms of *Leaving the mind alone*, this means to just relax, if thoughts come, let them come, and then let them go again. Thoughts will naturally dissipate if we don't engage with them or get swept up by them. Thoughts are like waves, they rise, they peak, then they break and dissipate. We don't have to do anything with them, just let them be. Thought is not a problem. Thought is the natural radiance of the mind, but like the radiance or rays of the sun, a little bit is good but a lot can be bad. We don't want sunburn. So, just allow thoughts to come and go on their own.

There are three traditional metaphors for the mind used to help meditators settle into the true nature:
- Empty like space
- Clear like a mirror
- Like waves dissolving back into the ocean

These can also be described as stillness, clarity (or awareness) and movement.

Object
All meditation needs an object, an object on which to place our awareness and attention. In our tradition we mostly use the breath, we just gently place our awareness on our breathing. The attention we place on the breath should not be rigid, it's not forced concentration. The attention we place on the breath should be light, like a butterfly landing on a flower. You will notice that awareness of the breath causes it to naturally slow (which is good).

If the breath is not your preferred object, you can use an external object, a crystal, or a nice flower or plant, or an image of the Buddha. If you meditate with your eyes closed, breath is the most practical object, but you can use sound, a pleasant sounding chime or the humming of a Tibetan singing bowl. Sound meditation sessions should be short, otherwise we might find we can't meditate without the sound. We need to be able to mediate in all situations. This is why the breath is a very practical object. The breath is with us wherever we go.

At first, the most important thing with practice is not how much you do, but developing a consistent routine. Meditation should be seen as an essential part of everyday life. Meditation will be deeper if you practice at the same time and in the same place every day. If during your practice you find your mind wandering, just gently bring it back to your breath. Thoughts will come, that's fine, just let them come and let them go.

How to Begin
Begin with short sessions so that you ease yourself in. Going in too hard and too fast might lead to abandoning the practice before you experience any benefit. You can start with as little as two sessions of five minutes each, separated by a short break of a minute or so.

In the breaks we drop our meditation posture, including our object of attention, but remain mindful, remain aware of our awareness. These breaks help us to take our mindfulness into the times we are not in formal meditation, what is referred to as post-meditation. Eventually this will make our whole lives part of our practice.

After a week or two, add another five minute session, and two weeks after that another session, so that you build up to 20 or 30 minutes a day. In time, you can reduce the number of breaks, to say one every 15 minutes and then one every half hour or hour.

The most important thing with meditation practice is that we do it regularly, each and every day, and that we accept that some meditation sessions will be pleasant and others difficult. Whether a meditation session is pleasant or unpleasant doesn't matter, every session helps familiarise us with the nature and workings of our mind. In that sense there is no wasted or bad meditation session, no matter how we feel about it.

The other important thing to remember is that meditation is a guaranteed method for recognising the true nature of mind, which is also the true nature of everything. That recognition leads to full awakening, to enlightenment.

PD

25 Please, Take A Seat

Introduction
This is a discussion about meditation for those who want to deepen in their practice. Rather than writing a scholarly work, full of quotes and references from fully accomplished meditators, I thought I'd write something from the perspective of a practitioner – someone who has been meandering along the path for a while and still has a way to go; no longer a beginner, and far from enlightenment, but somewhere in-between. I write from my own personal experience of what has worked for me and what benefits I have seen in my own life, and maybe this can be of benefit to others.

To begin with, we might ask, why meditate at all? The answer is simple and obvious: To be free from all mental suffering and achieve total enlightenment. This answer, however, might not sustain you for long when the daily grind of meditating sets in, and you start to think: Is this really worth the hassle? Life feels so very long when you are sitting on the cushion every day. All those hours can begin to feel tedious and boring, so you need to look at the big picture and the little picture at the same time. The big picture is achieving enlightenment. The little picture is that, month by month, year by year, you will start to see your mind slowly changing for the better. All those hours of boredom and frustration and impatience—and all the other difficult emotions we grapple with at the start—begin to dissolve after a certain point, and we start to see the kernels of benefit.

We see ourselves developing perseverance that we didn't

know we had. We start to realise that we are up to the challenge of looking at our minds, and all the horrors and joys that it shows us. We start to experience how impermanent and constantly changing our minds are, which as a beginner seems unbearable. When you get further along, however, this can become a source of comfort. The comfort comes from knowing that everything will pass. Everything bad that you experience will pass. Even the memories of those experiences will fade to nothing. This is something we learn on the cushion that translates directly into comfort in our daily lives. The comfort of knowing that no matter how bad our thoughts are, they will always change.

Getting Started
So, how do we start? We start in exactly the same way that all the Buddhas and masters began: By just sitting down, closing our eyes and observing the mind. Every single enlightened being took this exact same first step. They just sat down and looked inward. The Buddha did it 2600 years ago, Milarepa did it 1000 years ago, and the Dalai Lama did it in the middle of the last century. The thing they all have in common with us, is that they took that first step and just sat. We all have the same simple beginning and we all have the same tool to work with, the mind.

So often beginners say: Those people are masters and Buddhas and I'm just an ordinary person. This is true, but at one point in the past they were also ordinary, simple people. They had to be taught how to sit. They had to be taught to watch the breath. They had to be taught to watch their minds. They began from the same point as you. Their legs hurt and their bums ached. The thing is, they kept at it. For thousands of hours they just kept at it.

When they were having good days, they sat. When they were having bad days, they sat. When they were tired, or hungry, or sick, they sat. They didn't make excuses and quit. They just kept at it and succeeded. They became enlightened. We have that exact same potential. They are flesh and blood like us, and they had the same uncontrollable minds at some point, just like us.

So, long story short – you've just got to sit and sit and sit again. It's not glamorous, and it won't make you rich or famous, but it will give you riches that money cannot buy – a sense of inner peace and well-being, a means of controlling your reactions to things that happen to you in your daily lives. It will give you composure in the face of all that life throws at you. How often do we see people in our daily lives who exhibit a real sense of composure in the face of suffering? Rarely, I think. But how wonderful is it to observe composure in others who are having terrible struggles? It is awe inspiring. This is what years of meditation will give you: Composure in the face of terrible tragedy, both personal and global.

The more you sit, the more you will experience not only the ability to accept and adapt to events in your life, but you will also begin to experience the fruits of what true mental stillness will bring. You will begin to feel a deep reservoir of love and compassion for others start welling up within you. You will begin to experience spaciousness in the mind that gives you a sense of tremendous well-being and great joy. You will start to see that mental discomfort and distractions have the same essence as all the positive states of mind, and that fundamentally they are all equal.

This equal-ness is revealed when we just sit and observe mental events without jumping in and getting involved with them. You will experience moments of freedom—and even bliss—that can never be achieved by any other means other than through meditation. You will feel your heart open up to others. Eventually you will feel moments of tremendous warmth towards all other beings equally, without prejudice or bias. These are just some of the fruits of meditation that you will experience if you stick with it.

Making meditation a habit

Meditation, like anything else, can be made part of your daily life by simply doing it each day for a few weeks. It is best if you can do it at the same time and in the same place each time. This builds a familiarity with the routine and place. Don't make a big deal out of it, just sit down without any expectations or hopes for good experiences. Simply sit down, close your eyes, and start with watching the breath. No big deal.

It's amazing how many daily routines we have to maintain our bodies, but very few of us have any kind of routine for maintaining a healthy mind. We routinely brush our teeth each day, eat three meals, shower, change our clothes, perhaps do some exercise, and on and on. When it comes to mental health we put in much less time. For some of us it's completely ignored. Just as we feel confident that we are ready to face the world after our personal hygiene and grooming routines, a meditation routine will give us confidence that we can face whatever mental challenges come our way.

Another important point is to not put off meditating until we feel 100%. Some meditation manuals talk about how essential it is to be feeling mentally clear and alert and energised before engaging in meditation, but in my experience this is completely untrue. The Buddha himself advised ill monks to continue to meditate, even when they were unable to rise from their sickbeds. If we cannot learn to meditate during times of hardship, then how will we learn to face hardships in our daily lives?

Meditation is called a practice because it is something we continue to train in year after year. It is a medicine for the mind. What kind of physician would recommend taking medication only when we are well? We must learn to sit when we are feeling a bit dull and sluggish and fatigued, and a bit grumpy or depressed or angry. By persevering, and sitting down each day no matter what, barring severe illness of course, then we learn to watch these difficult states pass on by.

By watching difficult physical and mental states arise, abide for a period, and then dissolve, we gain confidence that when these circumstances arise in our daily lives, we can cope. As long as we avoid sitting with difficult situations, we will remain vulnerable to them in our everyday lives, and this is not the ultimate goal. Ultimately, we would like to be able to experience unpleasant states and not be completely derailed by them. By watching the mind and body constantly changing through good and bad states we will gain strong confidence in our hearts and minds that we can indeed cope with whatever challenges life throws at us. We will gain mental strength and agility and life will become easier and eventually more filled with joy.

Inspiration
Maintaining inspiration on a daily basis is difficult to start with, so having some inspiring objects in your meditation space is helpful. For me, I find having pictures of modern day meditation masters very motivating. These are not beings featured in stories from centuries or millennia ago, but masters who very recently, or even right now, have walked the path and accomplished its results. Many people have pictures of His Holiness the Dalai Lama, who has become a universal figure for peace and enlightenment. Another tremendously inspiring living meditation master is the western nun Jetsunma Tenzin Palmo, who, after living for 6 years in a small isolated Himalayan nunnery, then spent another 12 years living in solitude in a Himalayan cave meditating for 12 hours a day. I have a photograph of my heart teacher, Togden Amtrin. Having pictures of these kinds of beings in our meditation place reminds us on a daily basis that realised or accomplished beings are not only from the past but from this moment right now. They are an inspiration to our modern selves. It's good to have reminders like this that there are still living meditation traditions and practitioners who are accomplishing the

noble path that the Buddha began teaching 2600 years ago.

Another incredible modern technology that can assist meditators of all levels and abilities is the internet. One can find all kinds of inspiring videos relating to meditation on platforms like YouTube. One can also sign up for meditation classes online and join online meditation groups. So, for people who find it difficult to motivate themselves to practice on their own, there are now a multitude of options to assist them to learn and grow their practice. Decades ago, many of us had to travel far and wide to buy books to teach ourselves how to meditate or to find a centre or group to practice with. I made a number of pilgrimages to Northern India. Nowadays all we need is a laptop and internet connection. So all excuses for not meditating have been removed. Now it's completely up to us whether we decide to take up the challenge and put the time in or not.

Over the years, I have also found reading the spiritual biographies of meditation masters very inspiring and helpful. They often contain little pith instructions or nuggets of advice that worked for the master personally but are not included in the traditional or canonical texts. There is a long tradition within Buddhism, and particularly within Tibetan Buddhist culture, of reading such biographies as a practice in and of itself. This practice works not only to inspire the meditator, but to inform and guide them along the path, using an enlightened master's previous, successful journey as a roadmap. These biographies also include detail of the individual and deeply personal ways these masters applied the teachings and did the practice.

This is something that is often overlooked in Buddhist literature – that each individual practitioner's path will be highly personalised. From the outside it may appear that masters from specific lineages were all doing the same things, but upon reading their biographies, or talking to them directly, one sees that the true masters always tweak and tailor the practices to work with their own idiosyncrasies, their own minds. This is a very important point that should not be overlooked. Although the path may seem well mapped out for every practitioner, one must continually look into one's heart to evaluate whether or not specific practices are working for you as an individual.

It may take a serious practitioner some years to find their own way of making a particular practice really work for them and to see the fruits of their practice blossom. If one does the same practice for many years but feels no lessening of negative emotions, or improvement in the way their minds deal with challenging situations, then they may need to step back from their practice and contemplate why the practice has not opened up their hearts and minds. Ultimately, if one is not becoming more open-hearted and open-minded, then the practice is not working effectively for the individual, and time must be taken to re-evaluate the methods for oneself.

This in no way means that a person should become discouraged and quit practicing. It just means that one should take some time to engage one's curiosity and self-reflection, and endeavour to crack their individual code in order to make the practice work for them and deepen their own understanding of their own true nature. It may be useful to discuss your practice with a fully qualified teacher if you feel that you cannot unravel or reveal the blockage for yourself. That said, your own natural intelligence and curiosity should be your first port of call when attempting to understand how or why your practice is not deepening and developing over time.

Another simple technique that many practitioners use, including myself, is to print out inspirational practice quotes or short pith instructions and pin them to the wall in your practice space. This is to remind us of important topics to contemplate outside of formal meditation sessions as we go about our day. Don't put too many up, or you may feel overwhelmed, just one or two quotes that you really want to focus on. As an example, I had the same two notes up on my wall for several years. The first one was "This Will Pass".

This was to remind me that both good and bad experiences are impermanent. The second note I pinned up was the question: "What is the Nature of Mind?" This is a question many meditation masters ask their students when trying to point out the Nature of Mind. Both of these notes gave, and continue to give, guidance, nourishment and inspiration to my practice.

Present Nowness
In meditation instructions, one of the most commonly discussed concepts is learning to be in the present moment. Not living in the past with all of its memories, be they good or bad, and not living in the future, with all of our hopes, fears and expectations. We begin to become more present by learning to just observe the breath, which is constantly in the present, and letting any thoughts arise, abide and pass on by without grasping at them. His Holiness Dudjom Rinpoche described this experience of being fully present in the moment as 'resting in the Awareness of Nowness'.

Experientially, when one is able to rest in this Awareness of Nowness, the past feels more and more like a dream, and the future has no effect on you at all, because it truly doesn't exist yet. When one finds oneself resting in this profound presentness, it is extremely freeing and comforting. It has a boundless scope to it. It's not like just being calm. Being in the present nowness is so much vaster. One realises after being in this state of nowness that time is empty. Thus the past need not bind or consume us and the future need not frighten or tantalise us. Being truly present has a multitude of benefits aside from feeling calmer and clearer in the regular sense. It has the potential to help us see mental and physical pain and suffering in a totally new light.

In terms of the future, by resting in the nowness one doesn't have to live with the sometimes overwhelming fear and anxiety about future difficulties and suffering. As most of us know all too well, the only thing worse than this current moment of suffering is the knowledge that there is another moment of suffering to come. And another, and another, and on and on. We are never free from the knowledge that the future holds many moments of pain and suffering for us and all other beings. By learning to rest in the Awareness of Nowness, we don't have to live with this fear and anxiety about future suffering that is so destructive to our peace of mind. We just experience this one singular moment, which is bearable and endurable. We can all bear one single moment of suffering because we know it is impermanent, it will pass. By resting in the present moment of nowness, we only ever experience this one single moment. This has the potential to imbue us with a great sense of freedom. Fully present freedom. Not freedom from experiencing the pain and suffering in the conventional sense, but freedom from the psychological weight of fear of future pain.

In relation to the past, one no longer needs to feel the weight of regrets, traumas and resentments. We no longer need to feel bound by the things that happened in the past that we cannot change. They are gone. The past is dead. By truly being in the present moment, by knowing with certainty that the past is truly gone, you feel a tremendous sense of relief and liberation.

The nature of mind

Discussion of Awareness of Nowness brings us to the nature of mind. The greatest inspiration for practicing meditation is the fact of the Absolute Nature, the true nature of mind. Although many great Lamas have written about their own experiences of the Nature of Mind and there is no need for a simple practitioner like me to do so, Pema Düddul has asked me, a nobody, to talk about my own experience of this. Thus, although I am not a Lama, I will endeavour to explain my own encounters with this "state", purely so that it might be of benefit to those struggling to take up or persist with their practice. I am not basing this discussion of the Absolute Nature on book learning, but rather speaking from my own, albeit small, experience. I ask for my Guru's blessing that what I say is beneficial.

Firstly, it is said that if you think you are experiencing the Nature of Mind, then you are not. This is because it is an experience that can only be described or discussed after the event. During the experience, there is no thought in any conventional sense. No "I", no subject or self that is experiencing anything. It is a state in which all thought drops away and one experiences complete, vast naked simplicity. A vast limitless open awareness without boundaries. There is a basic pure awareness, but this is without a knower encountering something that is being known. It has a sense of great clarity, not at all a dull nothingness. It has a fullness to it. A vast potentiality. A vast open potentiality that is accompanied by a sense of luminosity. Having said this, there are no words or ways to describe it that can give a true account of it. Verbal descriptions can never do it justice. Words pale in relation to the experience.

It may happen that you have this experience in the presence of a Lama who is pointing out the experience of the true nature in order to lead the practitioner to it, or it may occur when you are alone, during solitary practice. There is no warning that the experience is imminent. It is completely spontaneous and unplanned. It cannot be contrived or produced. It either occurs or it does not. There is no schedule or timeline for the experience to occur. Although a practitioner may have been meditating for many years, there is no guarantee that it will happen at a particular point on the path.

Although an experience of the Absolute Nature cannot be produced or fabricated, we can create the conditions which make the experience more likely. By developing and deepening our mental calmness and stillness through meditation, we help to create a more conducive ground from which the experience will naturally emerge. Outside of our sitting meditation periods, we can also prepare ourselves by contemplating topics such as impermanence, emptiness and unbound compassion, all of which assist in undermining the strong sense of a permanent and solid Self. This belief in the Self as permanent and real is the main barrier to experiencing the Absolute Nature.

The main thing that can be said about the experience of the nature of mind is that when you have truly experienced it, you know it in your heart. If you are in the presence of a Lama who is pointing out the Nature, they may ask you afterwards for your account of it, in order to ascertain whether the practitioner has experienced it or not. In my case, I experienced it alone, without ever receiving pointing out instructions from a Lama. I later described the experience to a fully qualified master in the Nyingma tradition, who confirmed that my experience was genuine. Perhaps I have said too much about this already, we are not supposed to speak of our practice experiences too much.

There are many subtle states of mind that a meditator may experience along the path which may involve great bliss, or visions of Lamas or deities, or great stillness, but these differ from the experience of recognising the Nature of Mind. These subtle states are expressions of subtle or deeper levels of consciousness, but still often have the quality of an *experiencer* experiencing something. There is still a subtle experience of the Self. These may be pleasant and awesome and tremendously inspiring, but they are not necessarily resting in basic, naked awareness. Therefore, through practice, one will learn to differentiate between these subtle, often wonderfully pleasurable states of mind, and the experience of simply resting in the Absolute Nature.

The most important thing to know is that this Nature, our Buddha Nature, is as close as our own heart and we can all access it. We all have the same profound potential to experience the Nature of Mind, irrespective of intellectual prowess or education or gender or social rank or religious/spiritual status. All one needs is a mind and a practice and teachers to guide us to it.

Once one has recognised the true nature, the task then becomes to train in familiarising oneself with this experience again and again for the rest of our lives. It is not a one-off experience that occurs only once in a practitioner's lifetime, but is the first in what will hopefully be a succession of experiences of the Absolute Nature, in which one glimpses the true nature of reality.

The first time is like putting a serious crack in one's sense of "Self". We now have absolute certainty that the "I" does not truly exist, and that there is nothing in the universe that has any inherently existent qualities. The universe, our mind included, no longer appears as solid, fixed and permanent as it once did. After this, our practice becomes something akin to pushing a wedge ever deeper into that initial crack, opening it up more and more; dissolving the sense of a small, separate, permanently existing Self over and over again. There are various practices that can facilitate this, particularly within the tradition of Tibetan Buddhism, but there is not the time to go into that here. These practices are taught by fully qualified Lamas, which I am not.

Homage to my Guru, Togden Amtrin.

May this be of benefit!

MJT

26 Joy

Make joy the heart of your practice.
Without it there can be no realisation.

The joy of practice will arise naturally when you give up
the wish to accomplish something, and just engage with
what you are doing in the present moment.

MJT

27 Informal Guru Yoga

This is a brief treatise on guru yoga from recent experience. First a bit of a disclaimer: I have not read anything on guru yoga in about ten years, nor received any formal teachings. I'm writing these brief thoughts down because a few friends have asked me to do so. I do it in the hope that it may help others in their practice. If these words seem worthless then discard and ignore them.

The form of guru yoga I do is very informal. The informality is a necessity due to my illness, which robs me of energy and focus. You might think, "Why is guru yoga important at all? Why bother with it?" It's important because by gaining some level of accomplishment in it, however small and brief, you gain certainty about your true nature. You know via direct, personal experience that you definitely have Buddha Nature. Then, because you are confident in your Buddha nature, you also feel confident you can achieve realisation in this lifetime. By accomplishing some measure of guru yoga you will develop confidence that your practice isn't just repetitive lip service that may be going nowhere, but that it really can help you realize your true nature and Bodhicitta.

Now for the practice. Firstly, it's important to feel like you can really relate to your Lama in a fundamental, basic way. It's good to feel that you have things in common, however superficial this may sound. You need to relate to their personality, life story, lifestyle, and external form manifestation. This is a way of approaching the guru psychologically, and helps your mind develop a type of trust, as flimsy as this may sound. It's like building the foundations for your guru yoga. You need to like them, because they represent the enlightened version of yourself. You should feel like they are just like you, except completely awakened. Read about them, watch videos of their homeland, learn about their culture and daily lives. Learn all the details you can to flesh out your understanding of them from the ground up. Begin with their outer lives, then learn about their inner lives and their spiritual practices. Read stories about them written by their students. Really get as much of a picture of them as you can. You should develop a great respect for them and an ever-growing trust in their methods and accomplishments. Ultimately, become a fan. The beauty of this practice is that it does not rely on your Lama actually being alive, thus giving hope to those of us whose Lamas have departed this world.

Next, sit in meditation and visualize them in front of you. Visualize and recall all the details you have learnt about them. Recall all the inspiring stories about them, and that they truly were enlightened. Then, imagine them coming towards you and merging with your heart. You may want to recite a mantra, like the vajra guru mantra, *Om Ah Hung Benza Guru Padma Siddhi Hung*, while visualizing this merging. Repeat this merging over and over, at your own pace, feeling all the inspiration that you have gained from your investigation of their life. Feel respect and faith in their practice, and their path, and its fruition, and call upon them over and over to merge with you. Eventually you will experience the Lama merge with your heart and he/she will never leave it again. You'll feel a great joy and bliss with the certainty of this knowledge. Your heart/mind will feel expansive and free and full of compassion. You will know, with unshakeable certainty, that you and the guru are now inseparable. At this point you'll realize, or deeply understand, that you no longer need to visualize the guru externally, because he/she is now inseparably entwined with your heart. Along with this feeling comes the certain knowledge that you truly have Buddha Nature, and that you can absolutely achieve realisation in this lifetime. As sure as you are that the sun will rise and set each day, you will feel inseparable from the Lama and convinced that realisation is possible in this life.

MJT

28 Being a Buddhist in Hell

Thoughts on the Australian Climate Fires of 2019[4]
Burnt orange dawns, blood red sunsets, searing wind, palls of smoke the size of Europe that block out sun and sky. Tornados of fire careening across a bone dry landscape, cities choking on smoke and withering under record-breaking heat, white sand beaches blackened by soot. Birds falling from the sky dead, half a billion animals burned alive, nearly as many starving due to drought. Hundreds of homes turned to ash, many people killed or missing. Is this not a description of hell?

Every morning I step outside to check if it's safe to open the doors and windows. For weeks the smoke from nearby fires has been so bad that the air quality in the small town where I live was the worst in the world, worse than the most polluted cities. Often I wake with a dry, sore throat from breathing in the fumes as I slept. There have been days when I've opened the door and the world outside was a haze of ominous orange. On days like these the air smells of ash and death. Two months back (yes, it has been going on that long) an out of control fire got within a mile and a half of our home. We were told to prepare to evacuate. My partner, a dedicated meditator who is in informal retreat and also has a serious medical condition, said he wasn't going anywhere. He wasn't well enough to go anywhere, he said calmly, and besides he wasn't about to break his retreat for anything.

---

[4] A version of this essay, entitled "Practicing in Hell", was published in *Tricycle Magazine* on *Jan 07 2020*.

Without a hint of melodrama he said the fire would just have to burn him up. Such is his renunciation and commitment to practice. Luckily, the fires got no closer. Every day for weeks we checked to see if our town was safe, if we were cut off, if the fires had finally been put out. But the fires are still burning, not close to us now, but close to many others. Each day we spread feed for wild birds (who are starving) and make sure there are multiple containers of fresh water for wildlife (who are dying of thirst).

This is the world I find myself in, along with all my fellow Australians; a world of exceptional horror and trauma triggered by climate change. There have always been periods in history, and in our lives, when the ups and downs of samsara take a steep spiral downwards, times of war, plague, famine or natural disasters. This time of monster fires and devastation seems well beyond that. This is not business as usual. It's not even samsara as usual. This is something else altogether. Our darkest nightmares have become real. We are living in a kind of hell. Along with the acrid smoke, we breathe in daily distress. We are either directly experiencing or witness to previously unimaginable and seemingly unending terror. What can we as Buddhists do in the face of this?

Nearly the entire Australian population is overwhelmed and in shock. They are also feeling incredibly angry at those whose decades of inaction on climate change have led to this catastrophe. The Australian people's tolerance for these closed-minded people (some of whom control our government) is burnt to cinders; like our forests, our farmland, our national parks. What is left in our hearts is mere ash and yet another fire, the fire of anger. Even for Buddhists the calm and stillness that comes from meditation evades almost all in the face of the wilful ignorance of climate change deniers and the immense suffering of people, animals and nature. Even those with significant meditation experience are finding this moment deeply challenging. Many are asking: "How can I meditate while the world literally burns around me?"

With such desperate need in the external world around them, many of my Buddhist peers' practice hangs on by a thin thread. A number of them have stopped meditating altogether. For some this is just temporary, while they step up, as they should, and do what they can in this time of crisis. Some, I fear, will never regain their confidence in the many personal and social benefits of meditation. The intense suffering of the external world is turning their attention outwards, over-shadowing the importance of looking inward, of inner transformation. Their practice is cut. They have mistaken ordinary kindness with ultimate Bodhichitta.

Like myself, every Australian has asked: "What can we do to help?" Many have dug deep. They are all helping how they can – by actively fighting fires, by rescuing animals, by donating to the firefighting services, by volunteering with wildlife rescue organisations, by giving to those who've lost homes and livelihoods, by feeding and watering wildlife. Every day I am moved by how brave, kind and generous Australians can be. Yet I also find myself worried for their long term well-being. Without the very practice that would equip them to deal with the suffering of the world, with death and impermanence, how will they ever cope, not only with this terrible moment, but in the long term? How will they find any lasting peace or happiness? If Buddhists abandon their meditation practice, how will all the other Australians learn how important and beneficial it is on both an individual and communal level?

This is why when my fellow Buddhists ask "What can we do to help?" I respond by suggesting we should do whatever we can to alleviate the suffering of others *plus* our meditation practice. It should not be either or. Making it so is succumbing to yet another dualistic choice that is characteristic of samsara and is a result of not understanding the true nature of things, our interconnected reality. It makes no sense to abandon the one thing that provides resilience in the face of pain and suffering at the very time we need that resilience most. Even if we were willing to abandon our own chance for resilience, it is unkind if not cruel to rob others of any useful example we might have set, any inspiration we might have been to those around us to take up meditation themselves.

Buddhist practice, in the long term, produces a deep calm and inner resilience that inoculates us from disturbing life events, even catastrophic climate induced fires. Perhaps more importantly, meditation better equips us to help others in times of crisis. Furthermore, Buddhist practice opens the mind, making it receptive to truth (or facts, those things as rare as white rhinos these days) and less swayed by feelings and uninformed opinions. This means we will not be duped by those who try to mislead us for selfish reasons and we will recognise the truth when we see it.

Meditation also makes us less prone to negative or harmful emotions like anger and hatred. Buddhist meditation, with its emphasis on emptiness and impermanence, severs anti-social behaviours like greed, selfishness and bigotry at the root.

Put simply, by transforming ourselves through meditation we affect a broader social change by ensuring that all our actions are helpful, which means we actively benefit those around us. By transforming ourselves, we transform the world, making it a saner, more compassionate place, rather than a place with pervasive suffering only rarely interrupted by random acts of limited kindness. Without meditation there is only fleeting, partial "compassion" prone to bias, which is not really compassion at all. More to the point, meditation is not separate to or other than true compassion. Meditation *is* true compassion, lasting unbiased compassion. This is what we need right now. This is what we as Buddhists can do in times of crisis. We can meditate. This is what we as Buddhists should do. It is our responsibility and obligation.

Of course we must help others in any way we can, but

we must sit in meditation as well. Meditation is the only effective way to transform the world. Change must start with us, with a peaceful inner revolution. Even while the world literally burns around us we must sit. Help others, of course, but also sit. We must find the calm and stillness that leads to the flowering of unbridled compassion; only then will we actually know how to help in meaningful, lasting ways. This is the true revolution we need.

Fight fires, yes, we must if we have the capacity, but we must also sit. Rescue animals, yes, we must if we can, but we must also sit. Give support to those who are suffering, yes, if we have the means we must, but we must also sit in meditation. Help and then sit. Sit and then help. These two should always be together.

To drop meditation in times of crisis is like watering a plant in a basement. The plant will survive for a while, but in the end it will die from lack of light. The plant is our chance for enlightenment in this lifetime. The sun is meditation and the water is ordinary acts of kindness. Helping others in practical ways will keep us going for a while, but eventually we'll burn out and our kindness will wither. As our kindness withers we are even more cut off from true compassion and so the likelihood of our realisation will wither as well. Only meditation and kindness together will give rise to the true compassion that endures, the compassion that is the expression of our true nature.

This is why our practice must come above all else, why my partner puts it above even life and limb. Meditation is the surest way to connect us to that true nature, the experience of which is a source of resilience, compassion and joy. So we must sit and help, help and sit.

Kindness and meditation together lead to the flowering of Bodhichitta, the awakened compassionate mind otherwise known as enlightenment. We need that enlightenment to save the world. The quicker beings realise their true nature, the quicker the world will change, especially if they awaken in large numbers. There is only one guaranteed way to get to that mass awakening. Sit and help. Help and sit. This is what it is to be a Buddhist, especially a Buddhist in hell.

PD

29 Reach Out

You may have many great meditative experiences such as bliss and visions, but if you can't be kind and compassionate to others, then your great experiences aren't worth much. Compassion is the active expression of our Enlightened Nature, so reach out to your friends and loved ones often, especially during difficult times, and ask how they are coping. Listen to their fears and concerns, and tell them how much they mean to you.

MJT

30 There is Nothing Greater

Dzogchen is the highest and most definitive path to liberation of all spiritual traditions, both Buddhist and non-Buddhist. Dzogchen, which translates as the Great Perfection, is just the name for this approach in Tibet. It has other names in other places and other religions. Dzogchen is profoundly simple, free of cultural trappings and, above all, incredibly swift. Through the Dzogchen approach we can achieve, in this very lifetime, complete freedom from the dualistic mind and its delusion of separation, and all the suffering that delusion brings to ourselves and others.

Dzogchen is very popular in the West, precisely because it is simple, culturally neutral and swift. Dzogchen's appeal as a profoundly perfect approach does not mean that we ourselves have what it takes to be Dzogchen practitioners. So what qualifies us to practice Dzogchen? A true Dzogchen practitioner must have no attachment or aversion and not be bound by the eight worldly concerns – hope for happiness and fear of suffering, hope for fame and fear of insignificance, hope for praise and fear of blame, hope for gain and fear of loss. Also, we should be aware of and honest about the reasons we are drawn to the Dzogchen tradition.

Dzogchen is the highest, most perfect approach, yes, but is our interest in it equally lofty? Or are we attracted to Dzogchen because we seek to aggrandize ourselves? Our desire to prop up our egos is not a qualification for Dzogchen, it is a disqualification.

Dzogchen is the simplest path, yes, and does not require us to engage with complex rituals and yogas, but are we attracted to it because our minds are equally uncomplicated or because we are lazy, because we just don't want to do the preliminary practices or the generation and completion stages of Vajrayana? Our laziness does not qualify us for Dzogchen, it prevents us from even approaching it.

Dzogchen is free of cultural trappings, yes, and thus is deeply egalitarian and applicable to modern life, but is our interest in it because we are committed to equality and are free of cultural bias ourselves, or because we harbour a subtle xenophobia, because we are uncomfortable with unfamiliar cultures and beliefs and feel put off by foreign practices and languages? Our xenophobia does not qualify us for Dzogchen. Instead, it cuts us off from it.

Dzogchen is incredibly swift, yes, and can free us from the deluded dualistic mind and all its pain quicker than any other path, but are we drawn to it because we earnestly want to be free of suffering or because we lack commitment and persistence, because we just want realisation now, as though enlightenment were a desirable thing we saw in a store window? Our lack of commitment is not a qualification for Dzogchen, it stops us from even getting started.

The swiftness of the Dzogchen approach is desirable for one reason and one reason only – it enables us to liberate ourselves in a shorter time and then help to liberate others. If we can begin our task of freeing all sentient beings from suffering sooner rather than later then, obviously, we can drastically lessen the suffering in the world. How marvellous! Why would we engage with other paths that take decades or lifetimes to accomplish when we can equip ourselves to benefit beings in this one in mere years? Dzogchen is great and perfect precisely because it is the most compassionate path, it is the path that swiftly equips us to serve the urgent need of others. That is what great perfection truly means, it means the full awakening of compassion in action.

If we are unsure if we are ready for the Dzogchen approach there is a very simple test. If our concern for others is in any way weaker than our concern for ourselves, then we are not ready for Dzogchen. If we are not ready for Dzogchen but still feel deeply drawn to it we should do the preliminary contemplations on impermanence, emptiness, compassion and devotion – the thoughts that turn the mind toward dharma and away from samsara – and establish a persistent and consistent meditation practice. These things are more than enough for anyone to begin with and are, actually, the profound foundations of the Dzogchen approach. We do these things and only these things until true compassion takes root in our hearts. When that compassion arises we will naturally move towards the spiritual approach or practice that is right for us. This is our task for now. This is what we are doing for the benefit of all beings. There is nothing greater.

PD

31 Karma And Dzogchen

This is a discussion of the approach to karma found in *some* teachings of the Dzogchen Semde tradition. There are many ways of understanding karma within Buddhism. There is not just one model of karma. We are often asked to expound on a model of karma that sits better with secular westerners than the deterministic one found in Hinduism and Tibetan Buddhism. This discussion shouldn't be taken to mean that this model of karma is the view of karma we subscribe to. We are able to hold multiple views of karma without contradiction because we believe deeply in emptiness. We also don't believe that every Buddhist has to subscribe to the same model of karma. That is dogmatism. Besides, the dominant model of karma, that it determines every aspect of our lives, was never taught by the Buddha.

Something we have noticed about Dzogchen in the West, and perhaps also in the East, is that it is common for those practicing Vajrayana to get confused when they come across the Dzogchen teachings, especially when they read or hear things that disagree with other Buddhists teachings. One subject that is very different in some Dzogchen teachings from other Buddhist traditions is the view of karma.

In the Dzogchen tradition we don't view karma in the same way some of the other Buddhist traditions do. More precisely, in Dzogchen the emphasis is on the ultimate rather than the relative. We don't emphasise the idea that there is some kind of storehouse in our mind, consciousness or awareness that holds karmic debts or credits from the past. For in reality, where is the mind to be found? If the mind cannot be found in any tangible lasting way (or in any way at all), then where could such karma be stored? Nowhere.

Thus, when we practice Dzogchen we do not adhere to the notion that good people will have good things happen to them because they are performing good deeds or have done good in past lives, and vice versa. Good shit happens to bad people, bad shit happens to good people. This is simply the nature of samsara.

The Dzogchen view of karma is actually more in line with the early Buddhist view of karma.[5] The Buddha's original, revolutionary philosophy was that the self does not exist in any substantial sense (recent neuroscience backs this up). Furthermore, what flimsy, ephemeral, illusionary self that we construct from our misguided perception certainly perishes at death. According to the Buddha's original teaching, as enunciated in *The Heart Sutra* for example, nothing exists in an eternal way, including the self. In Buddhism there is no everlasting soul or consciousness. If the self does not exist, how can karma— which is meant to accrue to that self—exist and persist beyond death? It cannot.

The word karma as the Buddha originally used it means *action*. It does not mean result. It is the very real process of cause and effect, proven by modern physics and described in Newton's Third Law: Every action has an equal and opposite reaction. As Buddhism places the mind at the centre of all things, this means that negative thought will lead to a negative action and a negative result. Conversely, a positive intention will lead to a positive action and a positive result. This is very simple and yet profound.

The law of karma also suggests that all things that exist or happen are dependent on causes. In this way karma,

---

[5] See Matthews, Bruce (1986), "Chapter Seven: Post-Classical Developments in the Concepts of Karma and Rebirth in Theravada Buddhism", in Neufeldt, Ronald W. (ed.), *Karma and Rebirth: Post Classical Developments*, State University of New York Press.

when understood correctly, points to emptiness, it denies the possibility of things inherently existing. Seeing karma as some kind of storehouse or attribute of a self that persists beyond death does the opposite, it suggests that there is something that inherently exists. This is contrary to the most important of the Buddha's teachings – the truth of impermanence and the reality of emptiness.

Given all this, karma is not something you can have, but is something that you do that leads to certain kinds of results right here and right now. This is profoundly liberating, as Walpola Rahula explained in *What the Buddha Taught* [6]:

> … instead of promoting resigned powerlessness, the early Buddhist notion of karma focused on the liberating potential of what the mind is doing with every moment. Who you are — what you come from — is not anywhere near as important as the mind's motives for what it is doing right now. Even though the past may account for many of the inequalities we see in life, our measure as human beings is not the hand we've been dealt, for that hand can change at any moment. We take our own measure by how well we play the hand we've got.

The idea of karma as a past life inheritance is more a Hindu idea about an eternal self that has crept into some Buddhist traditions. Nevertheless, karma is a force to be reckoned with. If we perform a negative action it will have negative effects, including for ourselves. If we yell at a colleague we will upset our colleague and change the way our colleague perceives us. To them we will become an "angry person". We will also start to believe that about ourselves, that somehow we are inherently angry. Once we are labelled by others and ourselves as angry, it is very hard to eliminate anger from our minds and our actions because we believe that the anger inherently exists and is an inherent part of us. This misguided and negative view of ourselves will cut us off from liberation. We will not understand that we can gain

---

[6] Grove Press [1959] 1974.

freedom, that our potential cannot be dimmed, that karma has only a relative impact. As Dudjom Lingpa made abundantly clear:

> ... where are the amassed effects of harmful actions? Where is their storehouse located? Examine the manner in which any harm could be done to the emptiness of mind, outwardly or inwardly, above, below, or in between. If you examine minutely the mindstreams of people who continually devote this present life to physical and verbal acts of virtue and those who spend their whole lives engaging in harmful actions, you will find that there is not an iota of difference in the minds of both types of people with respect to the perpetuation of attachment and aversion, hope and fear. If they gain freedom, they gain freedom because their mindstreams are freed. If they are confused, they are confused because their mindstreams are confused.[7]

In Dzogchen we are encouraged to see everything that happens, good things, neutral things, and bad things, as the true nature of mind (rigpa) rising, abiding and dissolving constantly in infinite variations; as the manifestation of emptiness, the display of wisdom. It's not personal, and it's not necessarily because one's "past life karma" made it so. It is just reality as it is. Longchenpa, the great Dzogchen master and preeminent luminary of the Nyingma school, taught:

> The actual essence, pristine rigpa,
> Cannot be improved upon, so virtue is profitless,
> And it cannot be impaired, so vice is harmless;
> In its absence of karma there is no ripening of pleasure or pain;
> In its absence of judgment,
> no preference for samsara or nirvana;
> In its absence of articulation, it has no dimension;
> In its absence of past and future, rebirth is an empty notion:
> Who is there to transmigrate? And how to wander?

---

[7] From Dudjom Lingpa's *Refining One's Perception* (Nang-jang)

> What is karma and how can it mature?
> Contemplate the reality that is like the clear sky![8]

The great thing about this view is, because we don't have this mass of karma to either purify or accumulate merit to overcome, realisation is totally possible in this lifetime. No need to purify negativities for aeons and accumulate merit for aeons before liberation occurs, as other traditions emphasise.

Dzogchen teachings say that we can achieve realisation in this single lifetime by simply recognising our true nature, our Buddha Nature, and training in resting in this pure awareness until we are no longer separate from it. After this point we are free for good. This is the profound message of the Dzogchen view of karma: there is no vast obstacle in the form of karmic debt preventing us from awakening. We can achieve realisation right here and right now.

Dzogchen teachings reveal that our Buddha Nature can never be tarnished or stained, and thus does not require purification. Dudjom Lingpa (1835–1904) famously taught that the ultimate nature of a murderer or butcher is in no way different from the nature of a saint, or of a Buddha. Our Buddha Nature is pristinely perfect as it is, and thus doesn't require purification or accumulations to make it any better.

According to the Dzogchen teachings we already have innate perfection. We just need to "blow the dust off the mirror to see it". The mirror is an analogy for our perfect nature, rigpa, our innate awareness, which reflects everything in front of it without being affected or changed. The dust in this analogy is not "bad karma" or "lack of merit" but an obscuration, an error in view which is our misrecognition of our own nature, our clinging to the dualistic ideas of self and other and permanence and separateness.

---

[8] From *The Treasury of Natural Perfection*

This is what we mean when we say "samsara" in the Dzogchen tradition. Samsara is no more or less than a misrecognition of the ultimate nature of all phenomena. Samsara is mistaking ourselves and all other things as something other than the luminous display of the ultimate nature. That is all. Dudjom Rinpoche, Jigdral Yeshe Dorje, put this most eloquently when he taught:

> ... your mind's nature is the ultimate nature of reality. Once you have concluded this with certainty in awareness free from all characteristics of intellectual mind's fabrications and contrivance, awareness nakedly manifests as self-originating primordial wisdom. Words cannot express it. Metaphors cannot illustrate it. It does not get worse in samsara, nor better in enlightenment. It has not been born, nor will it come to an end. It has not been liberated, nor deluded. It does not exist, nor not exist. Awareness is unlimited and impartial.[9]

In Dzogchen when we say "merit" we mean capability to recognise one's own nature, so any practice that increases that capability is said to be increasing merit, but it is not merit as perceived in other practice systems. It is not some mystical power created by doing good deeds. It is simply becoming familiar with one's own nature and recognising the emptiness of self and other and the interconnectedness or oneness of all things.

When we say "karma" in Dzogchen we mean any habitual tendency that distracts us from resting in our pure nature and recognising the true nature of experience. Some people choose to believe that these habits are the karma of past lives, some that these habits are merely the habits that all sentient beings are prone to due to the misrecognition of their nature which has nothing to do with the past or the future but the forever present.

---

[9] From Dudjom Rinpoche's *Wisdom Nectar: Dudjom Rinpoche's Heart Advice*

In the end it doesn't matter what you believe because the solution to the problem of these habitual tendencies is the same: resting in one's own nature. Resting in one's nature extinguishes all karma and produces every possible merit or capability. Resting in one's nature clarifies all confusion and reveals the truth of all things, the truth of karma and merit, of emptiness and impermanence, and of interconnectedness and compassion.

This does not mean that we disregard the irrefutable law of action and reaction, which is what karma is truly about. It means that we have an understanding of karma that places the emphasis on the now, on this life and our behaviour in this very moment. We live ethically not because we fear some retribution in this or a future life. We act ethically because, on the ultimate level, acting otherwise is contrary to our true nature and because, when we rest in rigpa, harmful actions are actually impossible. Rather than weakening our commitment to ethical conduct, this understanding of karma deepens it.

Remember, all this concerns the ultimate, not the relative. On the relative level karma is said to still function. This may seem like a paradox but that is only from our perspective as ordinary sentient beings. Karma is said to be the reality for those who misrecognise the truth of their own nature, which is most sentient beings. In a way, karma is real for those who believe in it. Also, the notion of karma is a powerful way to encourage people to live ethically and do their best to avoid harmful actions whilst simultaneously motivating them to be of benefit to others. In this sense the notion of karma is very important and has been a transformative idea in many cultures across history. In our modern times we still seem to need a motivation to not harm others. Those without such a motivation are more likely to hurt others and commit acts of violence.

In ancient times the notion of karma also helped to explain things that could not otherwise be understood (such as congenital disease and natural disasters) in a way that encouraged resilience rather than hopelessness. These days our knowledge of DNA, weather patterns and seismology give us understanding of these things but somehow do not encourage the same resilience. To put it simply, the teaching of karma should not be discarded as mere superstition, even if we are drawn to the practice style of Dzogchen.

The Dzogchen style of practice is easier said than done, certainly, but it is definitely achievable. The Buddha Nature of each and every being qualifies them to practice in this way. Realisation in one lifetime is a real possibility. Once you have a certain amount of practice experience it will become clear that this is the case. At that point you will have no doubt about your own potential for awakening.

So, how can we begin to practice in this way? Although our Buddha Nature qualifies us to enter the Dzogchen way, we cannot dive straight in. In the same sense that a student might have the scores they need to gain entry into a medical degree, they can't start dealing with patients until they have the knowledge and experience they need. True Dzogchen practice begins with recognition of the nature of mind. Until we have recognised the nature, actually experienced it not merely understood it intellectually, we cannot say we are Dzogchen practitioners. Many think they are Dzogchen practitioners but few are correct. To get to that starting point of recognising the true nature we need a method.

We start with simple silent sitting practice, Shamatha and Vipassana, and what are called the common preliminaries. The common preliminaries are contemplations that reveal the true nature of our existence. They provide the view or perspective needed as supports for the practice of meditation. In the Dzogchen tradition there are seven of these contemplations that are best performed one after the other. They are referred to as common because they are essential for all and universally beneficial, not because they are not profound or powerful. In fact, the common preliminaries teamed with meditation practice is enough to take us to recognition of the true nature, if we are diligent.

As meditation practice and the preliminary contemplations are essential to prepare the ground for future Dzogchen practice it is paramount that we put all our effort into them. As well as familiarising us with the true nature of phenomena and our experience, the preliminary contemplations protect us from the two risks of Dzogchen style practice: the twinned extremes of nihilism and eternalism. Nihilism is a form of ignorance (a misrecognition of the nature of things) and manifests in the practitioner who allows it to take hold as a coldness of heart, a lack of empathy and compassion for others. Eternalism is another form of ignorance that manifests mostly as arrogance, as a superiority complex that bolsters the deluded sense of self and blocks any deep realisation of emptiness. Someone who thinks they are a Dzogchenpa with no renunciation and without having realised the truth of impermanence and emptiness is a deluded being prone to harming others and themselves, they are in a very unfortunate state. This is why Padmasambhava, who firmly established Buddhism and Dzogchen in Tibet, taught:

> Though your view is as vast as the sky, your conduct should be as fine as sifted barley flour.

The view Padmasambhava mentions here is the Dzogchen view, which is unbiased, impartial, vast and as unlimited as the sky; with no clinging to conceptions of samsara or nirvana, good or bad. Our conduct or behaviour, however, should be as ethical and refined as possible.

A Dzogchenpa has fully realised emptiness and so has no attachment to sense pleasures or anything in the world. They do not chase pleasure nor flee from pain. They seek nothing from the mundane world and wish only to practice dharma. They have given rise to boundless Bodhichitta and so never harm others and put all others before themselves. They have the deepest renunciation which is total non-attachment.

Until we reach that state of total non-attachment we must live in accordance with a strict code of ethics. We should completely abandon what is harmful and fully embrace what is beneficial. To protect ourselves from the two extremes and ensure we do not harm others and ourselves, which will prevent perfect awakening, we need to make meditation and the preliminary contemplations our new life-habits, our new karma. We must also have an ethical conduct above reproach.

We must practice these methods until we are ready to truly enter the Dzogchen way. How will we know we are ready? We will know we are ready to enter the Dzogchen way when we have recognised the nature of mind and realised and internalised the truth of the preliminary contemplations.

May what we have written here be of benefit. May all beings abide permanently in the bliss of the Great Perfection. Om Ah Hung.

PD & MJT

32 Cutting Through Pain

For those of you with chronic pain, this is a short practice on releasing pain that works for me. This practice comes in two versions, a conceptual and a more non-conceptual version. I'll share it with you as I do it, but you should tailor it to your own mind and needs. I start with some deep breathing, like the 4-7-8 technique. Next, I let my mind relax and settle itself into a relatively calm state. There are no time limits on this part. It might take 5 minutes, or 25 minutes or longer. It's up to you. Then I gently think to myself, "Dissolve all into Emptiness..." and just rest my mind. At this point, depending on your minds state, your mind may become very open and clear and free and your physical and mental pain may dissolve naturally without any more instruction. This is the non-conceptual version of the practice, where you are essentially resting in your true nature and all pain dissolves naturally of its own accord without any more direction or fabrication.

The conceptual version starts after you tell yourself to "Dissolve all into Emptiness..." and rest a minute. If your mind does not dissolve naturally into your true nature, then say to yourself one of these: "Fatigue is just a sensation", "Pain is just a sensation", "Anxiety is just a sensation". You can tailor those aphorisms to your own needs. Slowly and gently repeat these aphorisms to yourself, leaving good gaps in between so that your mind can accept the truth of this in a gentle, natural way, without any force. Leaving gaps is the most important part in the conceptual version, as your dualistic mind may still dissolve into emptiness during this process. If that happens, you rest in the radiant openness and sense of well-being and allow your pain to dissolve away. Even if your mind is too tired, distracted, or distressed to dissolve fully, this conceptual practice can still be very calming and helpful. In my experience, just by doing this mindfulness and awareness practice, it still reduces pain.

Even on days when pain is very bad, really awful days, I find this practice beneficial. Just slowly examine the pain. Ask yourself: Has the pain come about through causes and conditions? Yes. Did it have a beginning, a middle and will it have an end? Yes. Have I labelled it solidly as "pain"? Yes. Having fit all these criteria it must be empty. Then ask yourself: Can I take the label "pain" off it? Yes. Can I recognize its impermanence? Yes. Can I feel its empty nature? In time you will answer, Yes. Doing this you will find you are able to cut through the experience of physical pain and psychological suffering, and release the energy of suffering that you were holding onto previously. You will feel brighter and freer, and a subtle cutting through of the emotions that often attend pain, such as sadness and hopelessness.

When I do this, my pain is liberated and inspiration and joy take its place. It takes some time and patience, but it does work. Ultimately, it is nothing but mindfulness practice directed at a particular phenomenon, such as pain and psychological suffering.

MJT

33 Sky Gazing

Sky-gazing meditation is designed to reveal our true nature and give us confidence in that true nature, our natural state. The natural state is effortless and totally open, like the sky. As Dilgo Khyentse Rinpoche once taught:

> Just as space can accommodate the whole universe – the mountains, continents, and so forth – the nature of the mind is so vast that it can accommodate the whole of phenomena.

Sky-gazing reveals the vast inner openness that is our true nature by focussing on outer openness. First, find a comfortable place to sit in your yard or by a window. Take up the seven point meditation posture you have been taught. Leave your eyes open. Think, "For the sake of all mother sentient beings I will practice diligently until I achieve enlightenment".

Now bring to mind the face of your heart teacher, remembering the vastness of their wisdom and compassion. Plead with them: "Sole refuge, please remain with me until I reach enlightenment." Now dissolve the image of your teacher into your heart. Be confident that their mind and yours have merged and become one. Remain in that equanimity for a while.

Then, gaze gently into the sky, into the openness of space which stretches to the horizon and beyond. Understand that your own nature is limitless like space, as vast and boundless as the sky. *Feel* this boundless spaciousness in your heart. *Rest* in this feeling of openness and peace. The natural state does not reject anything. The natural state does not cling to anything. Thus, allow the gaze, the mind and the heart to be open to everything by not fixating on anything or rejecting anything. Simply embrace openness with warmth and enthusiasm. In this way you will see the face of pristine awareness.

When indoors or on cloudy days, close your eyes and imagine you are floating in open, luminous space. Feel the vastness and peace of that space, which is the same as your true nature. *Feel* it in your *heart*.

The true nature of mind, naked awareness, is open and calm like the sky. Thoughts will come, they are the radiance of the true nature of mind; just as sunbeams are the radiance of the sun. Both the nature of mind and any thoughts that arise are the same in their nature. Just let thoughts come and then let them go of their own accord. Pay no heed to them. Just rest. Rest joyfully in the calm and luminous openness of sky-like mind.

PD

34 No Expectations

When you sit down to meditate, do so without any hopes or expectations. There is no such thing as a bad meditation session. As long as you are sitting, you are learning about the mind, and this is an accomplishment you should be proud of and gain confidence from. Do not cling to passing thoughts, or pleasant or unpleasant experiences. Just simply sit and let it all come and go. We are not trying to get somewhere. There is nowhere to go.

MJT

35 Getting Unstuck: Troubleshooting for Committed Buddhist Practitioners

Introduction - Over the years many of our fellow practitioners have expressed to us that their practice had stalled and was not deepening. A number of these practitioners told us that they felt "stuck" – that they had been practicing for years, sometimes decades, without any sign of real progress. This advice is a response to that issue.

First of all, it is important to determine if we are truly stuck or simply *feel* stuck because our expectations of what our spiritual journey will be like are unreasonable or fanciful. Many of those involved in Vajrayana Buddhism are focused on outer signs and extraordinary accomplishments. In the Tibetan system there is a lot of focus on miracles, inexplicable powers and extraordinary occurrences. As a result, many of us expect our spiritual journey to be filled with moments of wondrous realisation and profound experiences. We are looking for spiritual fireworks, blazing signposts that show us that we are moving closer to final and full awakening. This is a mistake. The true miracle is the transformation of the human heart, the movement away from self-cherishing towards compassion and loving-kindness. If you want to know if your practice is working, simply reflect on whether or not you are becoming kinder. Also, we should determine if our minds are becoming less reactive, more relaxed and calmer. These are the true signs of spiritual accomplishment.

Getting Unstuck - If we find after years of practice that we are not getting calmer, kinder and more relaxed then it is worth looking into why this is the case. At this point we suggest that practitioners who feel stuck use honest self-reflection and contemplation in order to find the gaps or holes in their practice. Until we know for sure where we are in our practice we can't move forward. In our experience, not having applied and internalised certain foundational Buddhist contemplations are the reason for practice not progressing. There is a long history of Buddhist masters suggesting the same thing, so we are not out on our own on this.

In Tibetan Buddhism, these foundational Buddhist contemplations or practices are referred to as the preliminaries. In our tradition, they are known as the mind training (or lojong) teachings of the Great Perfection. These preliminaries have been taught by many great masters. The text we rely on for these teachings is Jigme Lingpa's commentary on the common Dzogchen preliminaries known as *The Steps to Liberation*.

To get unstuck and deepen in practice we suggest these preliminaries be taken seriously. In other words they should become our only practice for a time. This means we should stop everything else we are doing and just do these contemplations. If we have tantric commitments we can seek permission from our teachers to put those aside for a while. At the very least, we should reduce our commitments to the bare minimum.

These contemplations are not preliminary because they are basic. They are preliminary because they are the profound foundation of everything. They are not common because they are not special, they are common in that they need to be applied universally. Everyone needs to attain the insight and experience these preliminaries provide. Without the insight these contemplations provide no practice or meditation breakthrough is possible. Thus, when fellow practitioners come to us for advice on this matter we recommend that they go methodically through the preliminary contemplations in order to fill the gaps in their practice, and in so doing work to deepen their practice and continue on the path to realisation and liberation.

The traditional analogy of a damaged boat trying to cross the treacherous sea of cyclic existence illustrates the importance of this contemplative practice. Many practitioners have sought out "higher" practices before laying a solid foundation. This is like being in a boat with marvellous sails but a hull full of holes. The practitioner is attempting to cross this hazardous ocean with a boat that is taking on water. The holes in the hull are the gaps in our practice. Once honest reflection and contemplation is done we can see that our boat needs repairs. Then, once we know where the holes in the vessel are, they can be fixed. Then the boat should float or sail easily across the ocean of samsara to the luminous shore of Enlightenment. In other words, it is only then that our practice will go smoothly and quickly.

In an ideal world, we would all have ready access to highly realised Buddhist masters who can see into our minds and point out the gaps and holes in our practice. As such masters are extremely rare or remote from us, we must use our own natural intelligence and curiosity to get unstuck. When we feel stuck we have to do a thorough appraisal of our minds and practice in order to patch the holes in our boats. This will require perseverance, ingenuity, patience and diligent effort.

We recommend doing the contemplative practice outlined in *The Steps to Liberation* in conjunction with daily calm abiding meditation (*shamatha* or *shiné* in Tibetan), in order to still the mind and create the conditions for the practice to sink deeply into our hearts. As has been said many times by many great masters of the past and present, true dharma practice is done in the heart, not in the head. These contemplative practices, as well as our meditation practice, should be done without heavy exertion, and certainly without any expectations. It is best to adopt a spirit of open exploration and relaxed effort, and not use meditation or contemplation as exercises to make ourselves feel bad or defeated. Relax into the self-reflection and contemplation as if stroking a sleeping kitten or puppy; kindly, gently and lovingly.

There are seven contemplations involved in Jigme Lingpa's text and it is recommended that they be done in retreat over three, seven or twenty-one days. If you want to get started straight away and can't go into retreat, simply set aside enough time each day to do the contemplations without feeling rushed. Contemplation works best when we take our time. Go step by step and, if possible, don't move on to the next step until some signs of accomplishment have occurred for the current one you're doing. The signs are different for each practitioner. Generally speaking, you will know you have accomplished the contemplation when you feel it transform from a purely intellectual understanding into a strong feeling in the heart. Trust yourself and have confidence. Have a short break of a day or two between each step before moving to the next one. The steps seem simple, but they contain the entirety of the Buddhist path – Sutra, Tantra and Dzogchen. The point is not to give these contemplations lip service, or think yourself above them, but take them into your heart.

Although there are seven steps in Jigme Lingpa's text, we will focus here on just three: Impermanence, Compassion and Devotion. These three are particularly emphasised in many preliminary texts on Tantra and Dzogchen, as these three components to fruitful practice are especially effective at cutting away the "self" and propelling the practitioner into the experience of resting in the nature of mind. These steps, when done correctly—with heart, enthusiasm and feeling—destroy the duality between the grasping mind and pure, natural awareness (*Rigpa*). Any sense of a separate "self" will be gone and there will just be the natural state, pure awareness. These three components of authentic practice really are very profound. Without a deep understanding of them, and taking them to heart, no spiritual progress is possible.

Impermanence – The truth of impermanence is ubiquitous. It is so ever-present that we don't see it. In that sense it is a bit like our own nose. Everywhere we look, we see, hear and touch only impermanent things. Sadly, we mistakenly think these things are permanent. There is nothing permanent or lasting, nothing at all. Some longer term cycles—like the cycle of day and night or the seasons—give the illusion of permanence but these are also temporary. Even stars and suns come to an end, go dark. Eventually our own sun will dim and then there will be no more cycle of dawn and dusk. Why be attached to material things that are so ephemeral? It is completely illogical to invest time, energy and emotion into things that will not last and cannot provide enduring happiness. Furthermore, every single thing we own we will lose. Things deteriorate, cease to function, break or are lost. The impermanence of physical things makes our attachment to them illogical and delusional.

Likewise, our thoughts and emotions are impermanent. Thoughts and emotions are like mirages; unreal things that exist for mere moments before they fade away. It is this mirage of thoughts and feelings that we identify with and call our "self", our personality or identity. Why invest energy and emotion into this "self" that is little better than a passing hallucination? To do so is illogical and delusional. Grasping onto thoughts and feelings as though they are real and lasting leads to suffering.

Also, all who are born inevitably die. This is an inescapable truth. Everyone we know, everyone we love, will one day die. We too will die. Though our own death is certain, the time of our passing is unknown. It could be in a decade or a year. It could be in an hour or in mere minutes. There is no way of knowing. One of the biggest obstacles to practice is the misguided belief in an inevitable tomorrow.

We put off practice thinking we will do it sometime in the future. That future is a fantasy that may never come. There may be no tomorrow for us. If we realise the truth of impermanence, we would dedicate our lives to the practice of meditation right now and not defer it for a moment. The most common reason for someone not practicing enough or not practicing diligently is that they have not realised the truth of impermanence. This realisation of impermanence cannot be a mere intellectual understanding. It must be felt. It must take root in the heart.

Some may think that impermanence is the cause of all suffering. This is untrue. Our delusion that impermanent thigs are permanent and our resultant attachment to them is the cause of all suffering. Indeed, impermanence makes realisation possible, as deluded mind states are also temporary and therefore can be swept away. Belief in a permanent self, or in lasting emotions, leads many to feel that they cannot change. This traps them as they are, separated from the wonder of awakening by their own delusions of self-permanence.

Impermanence is not a negative. Indeed, it can help us to see and appreciate beauty. We appreciate rainbows all the more because they are so temporary. Without the change made possible by the impermanence of all things there would be no butterflies, no flowers and no sun showers. Most importantly, without realising the truth of impermanence and the renunciation it inspires there is no Enlightenment. Therefore, take time to deeply contemplate impermanence and take the truth of it to heart.

Compassion – In previous chapters, we discussed the fact that compassion is the ground, the path and the fruit of the Buddhist path. It is the ground in that our true nature is ultimate compassion (Bodhichitta). It is only this true nature that enables us to become enlightened in the first place. Compassion is the path in that it is a major component of our practice. By engaging in acts of compassion and loving kindness we connect directly with our true nature, reducing our own suffering and confusion, which in turn better equips us to assist others.

To be of true benefit we need Bodhichitta or "ultimate compassion", which is boundless and unbiased. As ultimate compassion or Bodhichitta is our true nature we do not need to do anything to generate it or make it greater. That being said, dualistic thinking keeps us at a distance from our true nature and from our natural compassion. To remedy this, we need to bring ourselves into contact with our compassionate heart by contemplating it, by understanding the centrality of compassion to our existence and the need for it as a remedy to the world's suffering. To connect with compassion consider that we only exist as a result of the kindness of others. Without parental affection and care we would not have survived beyond infancy. Some of us have difficult relationships with our parents but we have to admit that our mothers or fathers fed us and kept us alive until we could fend for ourselves. No matter how flawed our parents may be, they demonstrated their compassionate heart by doing this and we are here today as a result.

We can also see the centrality of compassion by looking at how sentient beings respond to it. All beings enjoy love and affection. Children light up when shown love. Animals thrive when given affection. It is a universal truth that all beings wish to be happy and none wish to suffer. As the Buddha said:

> All beings tremble before danger, life is dear to all. When we considers this, we do not kill or cause to kill. Whosoever tries to find happiness through hurting other beings, will not find happiness.

Compassion is readily ignited when we think about the suffering of sentient beings. For this reason, we should not turn away from the truth of suffering. We should not shrink from understanding the depths of misery that many beings endure in this world. We should not look away from the pain and anguish of the poor and oppressed, the ill and aged, victims of war and violence, or animals tortured and slaughtered for their meat. As Jigme Lingpa writes in his autobiography on seeing sheep lined up for slaughter:

> Seeing and hearing the killing of these beings ... caused me great suffering. I wanted to immediately liberate these beings from their suffering, and wished that I had a safe house to protect them. Such horrific activities occur merely because it was the season for slaughtering animals. Thinking like this, uncontrived compassion arose. Until that day, even though I had recited the words of the mind-training of the Four Immeasurables hundreds of thousands of times, I had never had true, uncontrived compassion of that strength. This experience was the most important event of my life.

Seeing the suffering of others and allowing compassion to arise in our hearts connects us to our true nature. Furthermore, as was discussed in the earlier chapters on Bodhichitta, when we practice true compassion—because it is of the same taste as the awakened mind—it leads to a realisation of Emptiness and of our true nature. Likewise, when we meditate on Emptiness, it leads to the dawning of true compassion. They are intrinsically linked; or, more precisely, they are in essence one and the same. This is because they are both coming from a place of non-self, a place in which the ego is abandoned. Therefore, take time to deeply contemplate compassion and allow it to take root in the heart.

Devotion – All the Buddhas of the past and present achieved Enlightenment through reliance on a spiritual teacher. This means that we must also rely on a spiritual teacher. As Dilgo Khyentse Rinpoche once taught: "The essence of reliance on a teacher is unceasing devotion, and the most effective means of generating and sustaining devotion is the practice of Guru Yoga." Jetsunma Tenzin Palmo once shared an old Tibetan saying with us by email: "Through meditation practice we *might* accomplish, but through devotion we will *certainly* accomplish!" She added that if we are practicing Guru Yoga and resting in the Nature there is nothing else required.

Some practitioners experience spontaneous devotion, they feel love for their teachers without any effort. If we are not someone who comes to devotion naturally, we need to actively give rise to it. It's important to remember that devotion should never be faked, it must be authentic. It must be a felt experience. For those who do not come to devotion easily, the diligent practice of Guru Yoga will give rise to it.

What is Guru Yoga? It is the practice of seeing our teacher as a fully realised Buddha. We visualise the master and dissolve that visualisation (which represents the teacher's wisdom nature, the Buddha nature) into ourselves, like snowflakes falling onto the surface of a lake. As the visualisation dissolves into us we understand that our nature has "merged" with the teacher's wisdom nature. The point is to realise that our own body, speech and mind are inseparable from the body, speech and mind of the Lama, of the Buddha. On the absolute level, the teacher is one with the nature of our own mind, which is itself the essence of Buddhahood. Through devotion to the outer Guru, the Guru within is awakened. The Guru within is our own natural awareness (Rigpa). As Yeshe Tsogyal taught:

> Meditate upon the teacher as the glow of your awareness, when you melt and mingle together, taste the expanse of non-duality. There remain.

Many beginner practitioners, and even those who have been practicing for a while, are wary of Guru Yoga. If this is the case for us, or if we don't have a relationship with a living teacher we trust, we can practice Guru Yoga with a teacher from the past, such as Guru Rinpoche, Yeshe Tsogyal or the Buddha. As the great Drukpa master Togden Shakya

Shri once taught:

> If you have devotion and faith toward the master, there is not even a hair tips difference if the master is alive or not. Understand that whenever you make a request to a master, you will always spontaneously receive his [or her] blessing.

Our teacher and friend Ngakpa Karma Lhundup Rinpoche once advised us: "Merge your awareness with your Lama and realise that the teacher and you have always been together right from the beginning. There is no such thing as meeting or parting. Let yourself be who you are". In many ways, Guru Yoga is learning to be authentic to our true nature. Learning from the root Guru, the teacher for whom we have devotion, even if he or she has passed away, is far more powerful than learning from any other living teacher because of the mind-to-mind transmission. This kind of learning is experiential and goes straight to the heart, whereas learning from the words of another teacher remains largely a conceptual understanding and does not penetrate deeply. Thus, even if our teacher has passed away or lived a very long time ago, we should not give up on fostering a connection with them as devotion to them will always be the swiftest route to deep, heart-felt understanding and realisation.

When we do meet a living master who we feel drawn to, it is important to spend time getting to know them so that we are certain he or she is a good match for us. Once we trust them completely, then we can practice Guru Yoga with them as the focus. It is useful to remember that devotion is not an ordinary emotional attachment or simple obedience. Devotion to the Guru is much, much more than just affection or love. It is love, yes, but it is also great respect, trust, faith and a feeling of awe. It is a heartfelt understanding that this being, the Guru, is our only source of refuge in this entire samsaric reality. It is not like loving a family member or partner or pet. It's so much more than that. No other being can take you from delusional dualistic mind to realisation. This is a very deep feeling and completely eclipses any other kind of love we've ever felt. The teacher is our true heart made manifest.

True devotion leads to deep and lasting transformation. The experience of devotion is awe-inspiring, blissful and transcendent. It utterly dissolves the self, leaving one in a state of vast spacious awareness. It brings forth blazing Bodhicitta and an experience of the ineffability of Emptiness. It is like seeing/meeting our own future Enlightenment right in front of our eyes, our own future Enlightenment made manifest as a guide to follow. On the ultimate level devotion is one and the same as Bodhichitta, one and the same as the true nature, one and the same as Enlightenment.

Although Guru Yoga is technically considered a preliminary practice, it contains the essence of the entire path, from Sutra to Tantra to Dzogchen. Some people think themselves above this practice, calling themselves Dzogchenpas or yogins and bragging about the fact that they are doing *trekchöd* or *tögyal* (the "highest" practices in the Tibetan Buddhist system). These people have entirely missed the point. There is no Dzogchen without devotion. There is no Enlightenment in a single lifetime without Guru Yoga. Furthermore, the dawning of true devotion through Guru Yoga makes practices like trekchöd and tögyal unnecessary. As Dilgo Khyentse Rinpoche once taught:

> Through the blessings that come from genuine endeavour in this practice of Guru Yoga ... the realisation of Dzogpachenpo will arise by itself from the depths of our being like the morning sun, and the meaning of the practice of trekchö and thögyal will dawn within us.

We do not need a formal sadhana or text to practice Guru Yoga effectively. We can do it quite informally. It is enough to simply visualise our chosen Guru—bringing to mind their compassionate qualities and wisdom—and then dissolve the visualisation into ourselves; making sure we rest in stillness after the dissolution. Of course, if we have a sadhana or traditional practice that works for us, then we can use that. The main point is to practice Guru Yoga consistently each and every day in concert with our meditation practice. It is also essential that we recognise that it is the surrendering of the self that makes Guru Yoga practice work.

Conclusion - Remember, we mustn't be too strict in our approach to these contemplations. This is not an exercise in punishing ourselves or making ourselves feel "not good enough" or inferior. If we feel we haven't accomplished a step after the three, seven or twenty-one days and are feeling frustrated, we can let it go and return to that step another time in the future. There is no need for formal sessions, we just make it part of our daily life. That being said, if we need the structure of formal sessions to help us focus then we should do that. Either way is good. All we do in the seven steps practice is remember the step we're on throughout our day and contemplate it.

We don't strive at all, we just gently contemplate the step we are on. By contemplate, we mean to *understand* and *feel* the truth of it. Feel it in our heart. It's important that we be gentle and adopt a warm-hearted approach. Some steps we will get through in just a few days, others may take longer, but we need to be patient, the time it takes doesn't matter. Our whole life is the practice.

Every Dzogchen master, even highly revered masters such as Dudjom Lingpa and Shakya Shri, such as our own Gurus Dudjom Rinpoche and Togden Amtrin, did these preliminary contemplations. Indeed, the greatest masters never stop contemplating these things. Why should we be any different?

JMT & PD

36 Meditation Traps

Do any serious scholarly study on meditation and it isn't long before we come across warnings about "getting stuck" in certain mind states, especially mind states that we interpret as pleasant, such as bliss and non-thought. Reading some of these scholarly warnings can make us feel daunted by the prospect of the practice. According to these texts it is all too easy to fall into states that are considered negative rather than resting in the nature of mind (rigpa) which is always positive. Spending our time dwelling in non-beneficial states that are blissful and enjoyable but not ultimately beneficial is clearly a waste of our effort. But how are we supposed to tell the difference between some of these subtle states without someone else being in our head telling us what to avoid and what's correct?

Too much scholarly study into what is essentially an experiential path can be a problem. A little knowledge is necessary but too much can deter us from practice. So what is the essence of what we need to know about these "trap states"? Fundamentally, all we need to know is to allow these experiences, whether positive or negative, to come and go on their own. All of the negative meditation states are experiences without awareness or with dulled awareness. That is one of their distinguishing features. So, a non-beneficial meditation state is being absorbed in the bliss or any other state such as non-thought without being aware and without recognising the empty nature beyond, within or in-between it.

If that occurs, and it happens to most practitioners, we can do a number of things to refresh our practice. We can simply reset our physical posture and refocus on the breath or we can do some Guru Yoga for a bit. We can also ask ourselves questions to help lead us in the right direction. Questions such as: What shape is the mind? What colour is it? Where does it come from? Where does the mind abide? Where does it go? What is the nature of mind? This analytical process is called "searching for the hidden flaw of mind". So, the technique is to analyse:

- Where a moment of verbal thinking comes from. What is its origin?
- The processes of verbal thinking themselves. How and where does a moment of verbal thinking abide or remain?
- Where a moment of verbal thinking ceases or disappears to. Where does thought dissolve or go to?

As well as that, when we are in non-analytical meditation, we pay attention to the spaces between thoughts. That is the space in which rigpa (the nature of mind) can be recognised. The point is always to focus awareness on itself, to look in-between verbal thinking and there we will encounter rigpa.

Most of the negative states described in scholarly works on meditation are also characterised by a lack of thinking, which in some situations is a good sign. The non-thought that is a problem is one in which the mind is sleepy or sedated. Non-thought characterised by open awareness is not a problem. If we experience the sedated kind of non-thought, and we might, we simply reinvigorate our awareness, our attention. We can do that by placing our attention on our breath again. Once our attention sharpens, we can place awareness on that space between verbal thinking, all without grasping or expectation about outcome.

All of the non-beneficial meditation states, if we don't grasp at them, naturally dissolve. Rigpa, the true nature of mind, lies beyond the dissolution, so always accessible if we allow the mind states and mental phenomena to just come and go. The universal instruction about mind states is "leave them as they are". We just maintain awareness on mind and its activity, specifically those spaces between verbal thinking. Having said that, the best thing to do is to just leave the mind as it is. The above techniques, guru yoga, focussing on the breath, analysing the hidden flaws of the mind, and others, move the process along if you find you need to do that but are not the meditation itself. Meditation is just leaving the mind alone.

If we feel daunted by scholarly discussions of these kinds of meditation experiences, perhaps we should stop reading theory for a bit. We need to allow ourselves to do this practice of meditation without doubt or fear. Ultimately, these states are not solid traps, they too are empty and will pass. A knowledge of and confidence in the emptiness of all things is very important to this practice. Trust in that emptiness and just observe as things rise and fall away again.

There are no traps if we allow our meditation to be whatever it is, without hope or fear, without becoming attached to the experiences. As they say, there's no good or bad meditation, just meditation. Focusing on either good or bad experiences is pointless, and a big waste of time. Just let them go.

PD

37 Simple Awareness

Bathed in rainbow light
Fundamental goodness unfolds
Outer and Inner
No difference
All of the same sweet taste
To Awareness

Simple awareness
- Nothing less than *Rigpa* itself -
Illuminates all
On which it shines its radiance

Nothing beyond it
Nothing hidden from it
Bathed in rainbow light
Everything illuminated
Simple awareness/fundamental goodness
Unfolds

PD

38 Let Me Let Go

For those who beat me
Let me have the highest hopes.

For those who steal from me
Let me have endless generosity.

Let me be a friend to those who hate me
And a comfort for all who do me wrong.

Let me not think of some as friend and some as foe;
Let me welcome all.

Let me be a good heart;
A generous mind.

May I not be afraid to have a broken heart;
To see to the pain of the world.

For all those who ultimately are my own,
Let me be free to love.

PD

39 Dharmata

We are the sky;
Storms do not tarry long.
We are the stars;
Clear light each and every one.
We are the sea;
Waves are our nature
Though we are calm beneath.
We are the creatures;
Those above, those below,
Those beside and those underneath.
We are each other.
We are darkness.
We are night.
We are sunshine;
We are the light,
And the vision.

We are the sky;
Never ending, limitless beauty.

PD

40 Home

Now, more than ever, it's of paramount importance that we recognise that "home", our True Home, does not exist outside of ourselves. It exists in the center of our hearts, and is none other than our Buddha Nature, our True Nature. These days, I hear many people expressing sincere distress that they cannot afford to buy a house, or even rent a decent abode. This is thoroughly understandable, and not to be taken lightly, but in light of the reality that so many cannot afford a place of their own, surely it becomes even more important to work towards experiencing the presence of the Buddha in the center of our hearts. Through regular meditation, and dwelling in stillness, anyone can access the experience of feeling this connection to our True Buddha Nature in the center of our being, our True Home. Once you begin to feel the presence of the Buddha in your heart you will recognise that chasing after a home outside of yourself is delusion, and only perpetuates your suffering. No matter where you are, be it in the city or the country, in a mansion or a humble cottage, by resting in the presence of your innate Buddha Nature you will always feel at Home and at peace.

MJT

41 Renunciation

Is progress in meditation, and in Buddhist practice in general, possible if you have a serious illness? Yes. I know this to be true from personal experience. A while ago I had one of those moments when the answer to a question that I only vaguely knew I had in the back of my mind came forward very strongly. I was relaxing, resting the mind, and feeling open to my Lama, Togden Amtrin. Suddenly I understood why my practice had gone ahead more recently, when my illness had been at its worst, and why it hadn't when I was younger and fitter. It was because practice had become life or death for me.

My illness had broken me so completely, physically and mentally, that I was on the precipice of either death or working towards realisation. There was no more middle ground for me. I didn't have the option of living a comfortable easy life like healthy people do, and forgetting my troubles by distracting myself with mundane ordinary things. My illness robbed me of any possibility of distraction from my present state. I didn't have the option of dabbling with a bit of occasional meditation while I lived a normal life. That wasn't going to be enough for me to live for. I had to put my entire heart and mind into my dharma practice and call upon my Lama for every ounce of help he could give me, or I wouldn't make it out of this situation alive.

I think this is the kind of decision one needs to make in order for swift transformation to occur. A live or die approach. This is the attitude yogis like Milarepa, my Lama and other serious practitioners have. It's all or nothing. They also didn't have the option of living a comfortable, cosy existence. They lived in total poverty and cruel climates and environments.

I am not sure if this kind of renunciation can really be taught but I am certain that without deep renunciation, no accomplishment is possible. It can only be arrived at by experiencing incredible hardship and making that decision when you are on the edge, that you will radically alter the way you exist or perish. When this world, samsara, has cut you down so low that you realise that there is absolutely nothing in it worth having, you either turn to dharma or lose all will to live.

I'm certainly not putting myself in the same league as Milarepa, merely using them as examples. The renunciation of those great masters is what fuelled their practice and propelled them forward. My practice is nowhere near what they achieved, but the same initial impetus to work towards realisation is there. I am not interested in anything samsara has to offer. For me, practice, especially deep surrender to the Lama, is the only comfort, the only possible solace, the only refuge. It is just me and my Lama now. There is nothing else.

MJT

42 Forgiveness

Forgiveness is not easy. It is also not a panacea. We need to do more than forgive to improve our relations with those who have hurt us or those we see as enemies. It is however a very good start. Forgiveness does not occur merely by saying it or thinking it once. We need to have the notion of forgiveness permeate our entire being. Like a rung gong, the feeling of forgiveness needs to resonate within us, throughout our entire being, over and over again.

For me, my ability to forgive came as the result of Guru Yoga, which may seem like an unlikely thing, but isn't. Guru Yoga clarifies everything and opens the heart to make forgiveness possible. Guru Yoga brings clarity and brilliance to the mind, and a positive feeling in the heart. When you are happily resting in that state, forgiveness can naturally evolve.

If forgiveness does not arise naturally through your practice, then it's good to work on it directly; especially if it is an issue for you. It is good to repeat an aphorism such as "I forgive you all". While repeating this statement, visualise all the people who have hurt or mistreated you, all the people you see as enemies. Repeat the statement as you see them in your mind's eye and allow your heart to open to them. Allow yourself to feel kindly towards them. Forgiveness is not an intellectual thing, it is an act of kindness and so must be felt in the heart. If you practise in this way soon you will feel waves of forgiveness to all those you are visualising.

If you don't know why you should forgive the people who've harmed you at all, then remind yourself that these people aren't inherently bad, they have simply behaved badly. They have made mistakes. We all do that. More to the point, they have not realised Bodhichitta, the mind of awakening that is imbued with boundless and unbiased compassion, so how could they have behaved any differently? They are trapped in the misery of the delusion of samsara and so are acting out. This doesn't excuse their behaviour, or make anything they've done okay, but it does explain it.

If we are not able to forgive people it is probably because we are focussing on their bad behaviour and using it to feel justified in holding a grudge. An understanding of Bodhichitta, and how bereft and anguished beings are without it, takes you beyond all that. If you understand that people act badly because they do not have Bodhicitta, and thus don't know how to do any better, you understand that they deserve forgiveness over and over again. At the moment this might not resonate with you, but as you practice you will begin to know the truth of it. One of the benefits of forgiveness is that being free of all our grudges feels great, as does feeling love for everyone you once disliked. This practise can also arouse Bodhichitta, the boundless compassion not impeded by the sense of self and other.

I for one pray fervently that I can recall this over and over again, so that I do not judge others due to their being trapped as we are all trapped. May we all keep that understanding in our hearts at all times.

MJT

43 Concise Dakini Guru Yoga

Above my head on a blossoming lotus throne,
Appears Dakini Guru Yeshe Tsogyal, the Queen of Great Bliss,
Embodiment of all the Victorious Ones.

Equal to all the Buddhas of past, present and future,
Guru Dakini – Queen of all siddhis, Dancer with Emptiness, Dispeller of all obstacles, Vanquisher of delusions and obscurations –
To you I pray: Inspire me with your example and grant your blessing,
So that all obstacles to enlightenment are dispelled,
And all my compassionate aspirations are spontaneously fulfilled.

Guru Dakini, from the four energy centres on your body of pristine light,
Send luminous beams out to dissolve into the centres at my crown, throat, heart and navel.
Through this generous blessing, I know that all barriers to full awakening have dissolved.
Dakini Guru, Yeshe Tsogyal, now please dissolve into light and become one with me,
So that I may rest in the inseparable unity of your ultimate nature and my own mind.

PD

44 Belief And Disbelief

I want to talk about belief and truth, which are rarely the same thing. We all have things we believe, and things we don't believe. Some of us may be surprised to learn that the most common reasons for our belief and disbelief in things is not the truth or veracity of those things themselves, but our own biases or our conditioned worldview. I want to address this because we live in a moment in history in which people criticise and disbelieve rather than explore and discover merely because exploring and discovering is harder and takes longer.

If we explore and discover rather than merely disbelieve or believe based on our assumptions or dogma, we have to abide in a state of unknowing and uncertainty for a while, perhaps for a very long time. We are deeply uncomfortable with uncertainty and so are quick to reject things we don't understand or that make us uncomfortable. Many of us actually think that something that makes us feel uncomfortable cannot be true or of value. This is illogical. It's uncomfortable to think that we will die one day but refusing to believe it doesn't make us immortal.

There is a strong thread of teachings in the Buddha dharma that make it clear that those who have experienced the nature of mind *know* the truth of reality rather than merely believe in it. They know it from their own experience, not from memorising dogma. They know it as a result of meditation and contemplation – which is the practice of exploring and discovering. Interestingly, the discoveries of present day accomplished Buddhist masters accords one hundred percent with the experience of all masters of the past. This is precisely because it *is* the truth. The experience of Buddhist masters past and present also accords with the wisdom of all the great mystical traditions of the world, of all religions, because all mystical traditions rely on meditation and meditation leads to the truth.

Even so, as Buddhists, we don't have to believe anything without looking into it first. Indeed the Buddha advocated we not do that, we not believe things merely because we have been told to. He included his own teachings in that, urging us not to believe even them without good reason. The Buddha advocated that we explore and discover, and accept and reject things as true or not based on our exploration. We just have to practice and discover for ourselves. The main practice the Buddha advocated for this exploration was meditation. Meditation is simple but not easy. As Martin Jamyang Tenphel often points out, 'meditation requires us to be persistent and consistent'. It also requires time, sometimes a lot of it.

Much of Buddhism seems strange to outsiders and beginners. When viewed from a certain (suspicious) perspective some of it can look like mere superstition or even blind, dogmatic faith. In Tibetan Buddhism, among the hardest aspects of the teachings for beginners to come to terms with are the teachings on death, in particular the teachings on rebirth and the bardo states. The bardo states are those gaps in-between living moments, the gaps between one thought and the next, one breath and the next, between sleep and wakefulness; the gap most acutely but fleetingly revealed in the midst of bliss. There is also a bardo state between death and the next life or rebirth.

All of the bardo states are considered powerful opportunities for recognising the true nature of mind and for ultimate enlightenment. The one at the time of death is seen as the greatest opportunity because in death the dualistic mind or ego completely falls away and all that is left is the true nature of mind that is one with all. A practitioner trained in recognising that ultimate nature through meditation merely has to ease into it when it arises in the process of dying and thus will achieve total enlightenment.

We can all directly experience and affirm the truth of the gap between each breath, the gap between sleep and waking and, in meditation, the gap between thoughts. We cannot do this with the bardo in-between death and rebirth, at least not while we are living. For this reason, the bardo between death and rebirth is the most difficult to accept as it requires a leap of faith, a step into belief rather than trust based on experience.

When I first began meditating at 18 or 19 years old I had a deep experience relating to these bardo states that profoundly transformed my view of the world. What I learned was that death is part of the illusory display of life and a great moment of opportunity. I had not read this anywhere or been taught this at that time. The bardo teachings include a description of the subtle architecture of the body (the channels, energies and essences or sa, lung and tigle). My experience reflected that description very clearly though I didn't know it at the time. Years later I attended a retreat on these bardo teachings. What I learnt in that retreat accorded perfectly with my experience, right down to the colours of each of the channels of energy in the body and the dominant colours of the visions that arise as you die and your consciousness falls away. I could not have made this up or known it any other way. There was no internet then, the bardo teachings were not available to me.

In other words, my meditation experience illuminated the truth. Death *is* an opportunity for enlightenment, as is every other bardo state, but death is most potent because the dualistic mind has been cast aside. All that is left is the true nature of mind that is one with all. This is why meditation is so important, so that we can realise the true nature of mind and then make the most of the opportunity for total enlightenment at the time of death. Without recognition of the nature of mind in our life we will fail to seize that opportunity. Only those who recognise rigpa (intrinsic awareness) can free themselves as the senses and the dualistic mind drop away as they are dying.

I do not need or want anyone to believe me. However, it would make me happy if those practitioners who doubt the truth of these aspects of the dharma simply remained agnostic until their meditation practice revealed the truth to them.

What matters is that we practice. Simply meditate, that's all we need do. We don't need to believe or buy in to all the other stuff. Things will make sense to us or not as we simply get on with it.

PD

45 True Nature Of The Mind

We are not what we think we are. We are not ordinary, limited beings. We are not our dualistic thoughts and emotions. We are not our identity or personality. We are much greater than any of these things. All those things lack substance. In fact, they lack existence. They are empty. They are just illusions. Our belief in them, our belief in an inherently existing self, is a delusion.

Our true nature, the true nature of our mind, is no different from, and in no way separate from, the Buddha's mind. We can awaken to our Buddha Nature, and dissolve our feelings of inadequacy, fear and distress, by applying some simple exercises. As Chagdud Tulku notes in *Gates to Buddhist Practice:*

> The foundation of our being is Buddha essence, Buddha Nature. All beings, whether large or small, have this foundational nature, this essential purity. Like gold embedded in ore, the truth of our nature—though beginningless, endless purity—isn't obvious to us. Because this is our foundational nature, we can reveal it through practice just as refinement reveals the gold inherent within ore.

These practices or exercises, however, need to be supported by a foundation of *understanding* which can be found in the myriad teachings on Buddha Nature contained within the Buddhist tradition. We need to first understand what the phrase 'the true nature of mind' really means. Then, with practice, we will have real *experience* of this fundamental nature that, with even more practice, will stabilize into what is called realization or enlightenment, the experience of oneness. But what is the true nature of the mind? The true nature of mind cannot be adequately described in words, which is why an experiential understanding is essential. We must encounter or recognise our true nature rather than merely be told what it is. As Dudjom Rinpoche once wrote:

> No words can describe it
> No example can point to it
> Samsara does not make it worse
> Nirvana does not make it better
> It has never been born
> It has never ceased
> It has never been liberated
> It has never been deluded
> It has never existed
> It has never been non-existent
> It has no limits at all
>
> It does not fall into any kind of category

Despite the impossibility of defining the true nature of mind, some pointers are useful in getting us heading in the right direction. Put simply, the true nature of the mind is simple empty cognisance, simple awareness that directly recognises the emptiness of all things, the empty nature of self and all phenomena. To recognise the mind's true nature, we need simply look at it, to place awareness on awareness itself. As Tulku Urgyen taught:

> Empty cognizance is our nature. We cannot separate one aspect of it from the other. Empty means "not made out of anything whatsoever"; our nature has always been this way. Yet, while being empty, it has the capacity to cognize, to experience, to perceive. It's not so difficult to comprehend this; to get the theory that this empty cognizance is Buddha Nature, self-existing wakefulness.[10]

---

[10] "As the Clouds Vanish", *Tricycle Magazine*, Winter 1999.

The true nature of mind is another phrase for the Buddha Nature and as such points both to the mind's unimaginable potential and the mind's natural qualities. Ngakpa Karma Lhundup Rinpoche refers to this natural quality of the mind as *fundamental goodness*. Dilgo Khyentse Rinpoche eloquently describes this fundamental goodness or nature of mind in the poem below:

> The source of all phenomena of samsara and nirvana
> Is the nature of mind;
> Void, luminous,
> All-encompassing, vast as the sky.[11]

Although correct view or understanding is important to recognizing and abiding in one's true nature, the true nature is not something that needs to be developed or cultivated. To free ourselves of dualistic mind and rest in the pristine nature—and thus be rid of all disturbing emotions—we need to follow a path of practice.

The path has three components: View, Meditation and Action. Understanding the truth of things as they really are rather than how we misperceive them is the view. The view gives us a sense of the pristine ground of our being that changes our deluded perception.

Meditation, which is simple silent sitting, allows us to rest in and stabilize our experience of pristine nature. Action involves two things, living ethically according to dharma principles and bringing the recognition of our pristine nature into daily life, so that we are resting in that nature (rigpa) all the time rather than just while sitting on our meditation cushion in formal practice sessions.

As we remain in that pristine nature for longer and longer periods of time, all delusion—all negative emotions and dualistic thinking—will dissolve of their own accord, without effort. That is realization, the fruit of the path,

---

[11] In *Rabsel*, Issue 5, Shechen Publications. Translated by Matthieu Ricard.

which is oneness with the enlightened mind of all the Buddhas.

The reason why all dualistic thinking and unhelpful emotions will dissolve of their own accord without effort, if we just rest in our pristine mind, is because these thoughts and emotions are in their nature empty of separate, independent self-existence; they are sunyata (emptiness).

Their nature is sunyata because they rise from rigpa and have the exact same quality as rigpa, which is also sunyata. The ripples and the wave are not different in any way from the ocean. The reflection of the mirror is not separate from the mirror. Buddha Nature is sunyata, sunyata is Buddha Nature As Dilgo Khyentse Rinpoche has taught:

> The infinite and inexpressible qualities of primordial wisdom "the true nirvana" are inherent in our mind. It is not necessary to create them, to fabricate something new. Spiritual realization only serves to reveal them ... Finally, if one considers them from an ultimate point of view, these qualities are themselves only emptiness. (Buddha Nature).

Through simple silent sitting meditation, informed by our understanding of Sunyata and Buddha Nature—which are, we now know, one and the same—we can encounter and take refuge in our fundamental goodness, rigpa, the true nature of everything. Khenchen Thrangu Rinpoche put it this way:

> So we meditate on the essence of everything which is emptiness. Through that meditation we will discover this emptiness has within it wisdom and clarity. Through the process of becoming used to the emptiness and clarity which is the universal essence or dharmata we will automatically eliminate all of the delusions which have been blocking that vision.

It seems too easy to think that this simple technique, silent sitting meditation informed by correct view, could be so transformative and powerful. This is because the true nature of mind is not something distant and unreachable, it is our very own awareness, undistracted by thought and fully cognisant of emptiness. If you don't trust me, then trust one of the most respected meditation masters of the modern era, Dudjom Rinpoche, who counselled us to focus our energy on just this one, simple thing:

> Although hundreds or thousands of explanations are given,
> There is only one thing to be understood—
> Know the one thing that liberates everything—
> Awareness itself, your true nature.

By recognizing and resting in fundamental goodness we can be free of all our limitations and unhealthy inhibitions. We can overcome self-loathing and doubt and mistrust. We can also overcome our fear and trauma.

Why on earth would we put energy into anything else? To do so is to be at a banquet and yet starve to death because we are too distracted by all the sights and smells to actually eat.

PD

46 Imminence

The more we allow the Dharma to penetrate our hearts, the more we feel the great potentiality within this Empty existence. The more we rest in the Natural State, the more we feel this imminence. This is Vajra confidence, which arises to show us that realisation is absolutely possible in this lifetime.

MJT

47 The Gap

Have you asked yourself today "What is the Nature of Mind?" Each time you ask yourself this question do not then jump in immediately with a conceptual, pre-fabricated answer, but leave a gap. This is very important. To ask the question, and then leave the mind be.

Leave room in your mind for wonder to arise! Don't suffocate your practice with too many concepts and expectations. Tremendous beauty, joy and freedom will emerge naturally if you leave space for it to do so.

MJT

48 Freedom From Disturbing Emotions

Everything in the universe and in the thinking mind is the illusory and empty display of the true nature of mind, which is boundless and open like the sky, like limitless space. That limitless openness is the ultimate antidote to disturbing emotions, to anxiety, panic, fear and grief.

To connect with that spacious nature of mind all we need do is rest in an experience of appreciative joy. The Buddha taught that without joy there is no enlightenment. Joy as a practice is profound and transformative, especially for those afflicted by disturbing emotions or trauma.

In the calmest time of your day, each and every day, do the following:

1. Sit in a comfortable meditation posture. Once settled, summon the intention to meditate in order to recognise the true nature and thus be able to guide all sentient beings to liberation. Then take a deep breath from the diaphragm to the count of four. As you breathe in, know that your heart and mind are being infused with calm clarity. After a brief pause, exhale to the count of eight. While exhaling allow all tension in the mind and body to fall away and all muscles to relax. Repeat this step three or four times. This need only take a few minutes.

2. Bring to mind an experience of stillness, joy or bliss from your past. It doesn't have to be a moment of great intensity, a moment of simple or subtle joy will suffice. Remember how that joy or bliss felt in the body. Allow that feeling to grow and intensify in your body now. Know that this feeling

is analogous to an experience of the true nature of mind. Rest in the feeling of stillness, joy or bliss for a moment, remembering that everything in the universe is the illusory and empty display of the true nature of mind (or *Rigpa* in Tibetan).

3. Now say to yourself: "everything is Rigpa" or "racing thoughts are Rigpa" or "anxiety is Rigpa". Afterwards, rest in the feeling of stillness, joy or bliss. Allow the sensations of joy to relax the body and calm the mind. This should take just a few minutes.

4. Throughout your day, remind yourself "anxiety is Rigpa" or "racing thoughts are Rigpa" and briefly summon the stillness, joy or bliss. Allow the sensations of joy to relax the body and calm the mind. This should take mere moments, no more than a minute or two at a time.

5. When not sitting in meditation and you find the mind is racing or there is anxiety, just remind yourself "racing thoughts are Rigpa" or "anxiety is Rigpa" and rest in the feeling of stillness, joy or bliss that this statement now summons. Allow the sensations of joy to relax the body and calm the mind. It will take consistency doing the first four steps in the calmest part of your day every single day for it to work in moments of intense anxiety or disturbing emotions. Trying to apply it in those tough moments without having practised it in calmer moments will not work well.

After each formal session dedicate your practice to the benefit of all sentient beings by saying something like "May all beings experience true joy and be liberated from all suffering. May all sentient beings know love and abide in the perfection of enlightenment."

To support your meditation it can help to take a moment each night before bed to write down all the things for which you are appreciative or grateful. It need not be a long list, just think of a few things. Also try to feel joy for others when good things happen and they have success. Feeling gratitude for our lives, even if they are very difficult, and feeling joy for others will liberate us from the disturbing emotions of dissatisfaction, jealousy and envy. Joy and gratitude open up the mind. Don't underestimate them.

PD

49 Simply Awaken

We don't need to strive in order to hear, we just hear. We don't need to strive in order to see, we just see. We don't need to strive in order to taste, we just taste. We don't need to strive in order to feel, we just feel. We don't need to strive in order to smell, we just smell. We do not need to strive in order to wake, we simply awaken.

When we stay in the awareness of the moment, not classifying, describing or judging what we sense, just remaining gently present, then we are truly aware, truly awake.

PD

50 No Meeting Or Parting

It is easier to sever a limb than be separated from one's own Buddha Nature. There is no separation, never has been and never will be. You are always in union with your Buddha Nature, and always in union with the Guru who is the outer, physical manifestation of that perfect nature. There is no meeting or parting with the Guru, we are always one.

MJT

51 Love Is The Ultimate Antidote

Love - pure, deep, heartfelt love for others - is the antidote to hatred and ill-will. It is the antidote to despair and anxiety. Love - in its ultimate form as Bodhicitta - is the supreme antidote to self-clinging and is the path to dissolving all delusion and neurosis. Vast limitless love for all beings, without discrimination, obligation or prejudice, is the ultimate freedom.

MJT

52 Joyful Journey

Whatever practice you do, approach it with a child-like sense of curiosity and enthusiasm. Each session is fresh and full of possibilities, so don't make your meditation a chore. Recognise that it is a great adventure that you are lucky enough to be on and continue it with joy.

MJT

53 Rest the Mind

Rest the mind, for in the absence of effort the True Nature is revealed. Samsara is entirely mind-made. All one need do to undermine samsara is to resist the urge to follow every thought and feeling that arises in the mind. We begin training in this in our meditation practice by simply observing thoughts arising, abiding and dissolving, all without effort. So meditate beloved ones, until your body feels as stable and immovable as a great mountain. Until your mind becomes as clear and still as a vast lake on a summers day. Until you no longer recognise the difference between meditation and non-meditation.

MJT

54 There Is Only This

Everything in the mind and the universe is the magical emanation of the ultimate nature; pervasive and pristine awareness, Rigpa.

All thought and emotion, all objects of the senses, all existent things, are mirages and dreams, rainbow-like illusions, luminous and effervescent, yet impermanent and empty; all arising from the clear light of Rigpa and inseparable from it, like the warmth of a fire or the rays of the sun.

When we look, we see only Rigpa. When we listen, we hear only Rigpa. We cannot taste without tasting Rigpa itself. We cannot touch without touching the face of pristine awareness. There is no scent but the fragrance of Rigpa. When we think or feel, we are experiencing no less than the radiant dance of the ultimate nature.

Everything is Rigpa's vast display. There is nothing else. No you, no me, no this, no that, no here, no there, no then and no now. There is simply the oneness of the natural state of emptiness, the ultimate nature and its myriad reflections.

As there is only pervasive and pristine awareness – and nothing further worth pursuing or experiencing – why not settle into the great simplicity of the natural state right now?

PD

55 Be Free In Naked Awareness

What is there to accumulate, and who is there to accumulate it? What is there to purify, and who is there to purify it?

Through contemplation and meditation upon Emptiness, we learn to throw off the calcified layers of identity and Self, and be free in Naked Awareness!

MJT

56 Empty Echoes

All thoughts and emotions, fleeting and baseless, are mere empty echoes, triggered by external events or the memory of external events, which themselves are impermanent and devoid of substance. Our thoughts and emotions are described as our "inner life" and yet they have nothing to do with our true inner life. We are not who we think we are and we are not what we think about ourselves. Not only do our thoughts and emotions shed no light on our true inner nature, they are what obscures it. Tragically, we are so focussed on our thoughts and emotions that we think they are the sum total of who we are. We identify with thoughts and emotions and misconstrue them for a self. We do not experience that which thoughts and emotions obscure, we are totally clueless about our true nature, our innate pristine awareness. To experience who we truly are all we need do is shift our focus away from thoughts and emotions, and away from the delusion of self they perpetuate. This shift of focus is so profoundly simple, yet it is something so very few ever achieve, mostly because they never even try. Once we have achieved this shift in focus, through simple meditation, and we are settled in our true nature, then we will experience thoughts and emotions not as obscurations but as the natural radiance of pristine awareness.

PD

57 The Guru Is Present Nowness

The Guru *is* this single moment of awareness. Not "like" this moment of awareness, or "similar" to it, but this actual moment of simple pure awareness itself. The Guru is not pointing to it, or symbolic of it, but actually *is* it. This I am now certain of deep within my heart.

When you realise this, all form practice falls away, and there is only a direct experience of vivid naked unadulterated simple awareness. Such an experience of the natural state, the true guru, is profoundly transformative. After such an experience, you are likely to weep with relief, bliss and joy.

MJT

58 It's Up To You

Wherever you plant your feet, may that be the line drawn against anger, hatred and violence;
Wherever you stand,
May only compassion, kindness and benevolence abide.

May your presence in the world be a bulwark against the tide of selfishness, narcissism and greed;
Wherever you are,
May there be selflessness, concern for others and generosity.

In the face of ignorance, closed-mindedness and egotism,
Show the face of wisdom, open-heartedness and humility.
May you become a light for those in need and a safe-haven for all.

If it is not you who awakens the power of compassion, selflessness and wisdom then who will it be?
It is up to you.
And if not now, then when?

PD

About Pema

Pema Düddul (birth name: Dallas John Baker) is the Buddhist Chaplain in the University of Southern Queensland's Multi-Faith Service and the Director of Jalü Buddhist Meditation Centre. Pema has been a Buddhist for forty years, discovering at the age of eleven that his personal worldview and the tenets of Buddhism were in perfect accordance. He has practiced in the Vajrayana, or Tibetan Buddhist, tradition for more than half of that time. Pema considers Dudjom Rinpoche, Jigdral Yeshe Dorje (1904-1987) to be his Heart Lama. Pema has received teachings from masters in all four schools of Tibetan Buddhism. In 2005 he received the tantric vows of a ngakpa, the Tibetan Buddhist equivalent of a non-monastic religious minister. He received these vows from one of his principle teachers, Ngakpa Karma Lhundup Rinpoche. It was around this time that he was given the Dharma name Pema Düddul. Pema has decades of experience as a Buddhist practitioner and has taught mindfulness and meditation in Buddhist, educational and corporate settings since 2007.

About Jamyang

Martin Jamyang Tenphel is an Australian-born Buddhist practitioner, meditation instructor and Co-Director of Jalü Buddhist Meditation Centre. He discovered the dharma in 1995 and then studied and practiced in Australia and India for the next decade, primarily in the Tibetan tradition. Since 2005 his focus has been on practice rather than study. His Guru is the late Togden Amtrin, a highly revered yogi of the Drukpa Kagyu lineage from Khampagar Monastery in Eastern Tibet. Jamyang was a monk for a few years during his twenties, but handed back his robes and later took the Tantric Ngakpa ordination with Ngakpa Karma Lhundup Rinpoche. Jamyang has received teachings from masters in all four schools of Tibetan Buddhism, though practices in the Drukpa tradition. Despite a debilitating and sometimes life-threatening illness of twenty years duration, Jamyang has maintained his meditation practice, using his sick bed as his retreat place. Jamyang's heart practice is Guru Yoga and meditation on the nature of mind. He lives in informal retreat most of the time, but is not completely cut off from the world. He occasionally reaches out to support fellow practitioners using modern technology.

Visit us online: www.jalumeditation.org
https://www.facebook.com/JaluMeditation